Neil, thank you from your Four Corners' friends.

June, 1996

THE GOLFER'S

COMPANION

An Illustrated Guide to the Highlights, History, and Best Courses, Holes, and Players of Professional Golf

JOHN DELERY

MALLARD PRESS

An Imprint of BDD Promotional Book Company, Inc.

666 Fifth Avenue

New York, NY 10103

A FRIEDMAN GROUP BOOK

Published by MALLARD PRESS
An imprint of BDD Promotional Book Company, Inc.
666 Fifth Avenue
New York, N.Y. 10103

Mallard Press and its accompanying design and logo are trademarks of BDD Promotional Book Company, Inc.

ISBN 0–7924–5463–4

THE GOLFER'S COMPANION
An Illustrated Guide to the Highlights, History, and Best Courses, Holes, and Players of Professional Golf
was prepared and produced by
Michael Friedman Publishing Group, Inc.
15 West 26th Street
New York, New York 10010

Editor: Robert Hernandez
Art Director: Jeff Batzli
Designer: Robert W. Kosturko
Photo Researcher: Daniella Jo Nilva

Typeset by Classic Type, Inc.
Color separation by Scantrans Pte. Ltd.
Printed and bound in Hong Kong by Leefung-Asco Printers Ltd.

Additional Photography Credits
Contents Page (clockwise from top left): © FPG International, © Otto Greule/Allsport, © David Cannon/Allsport, © David Cannon/Allsport, © Allsport, © Bob Thomas Sports Photography

To Mom and Dad, who taught me everything I know about life;
now if only one of you could teach me how to putt, I'd call you perfect parents.

Acknowledgements

Thanks to some true golf professionals; the people who provide information for the Ladies Professional Golf Association, the Professional Golfers Association, and the United States Golf Association, especially Robert Sommers; Greg Garber, Hank Gola, Abbott Koloff, and Bill Varner, all good writers and good friends; Mike Tschappat, whose judgment I seek and trust; editors Sharon Kalman and Robert Hernandez of the Michael Friedman Publishing Group for their assistance and expertise.

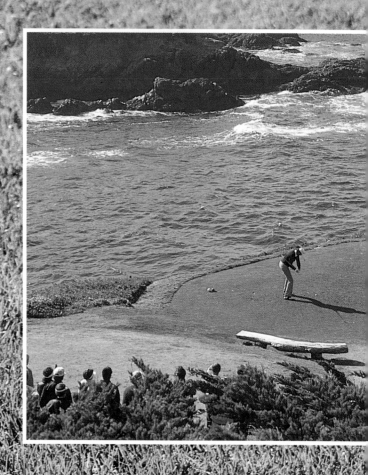

CONTENTS

The Game of Golf

Golf backward is flog—absolute evidence that golf is not an amusing game, but rather an inhuman form of torture. Pain and golf are a matched set.

"No one ever, ever masters golf," says Gary Player of South Africa, whose success in the sport—he has won more than 130 professional tournaments since 1954—contradicts his dismal declaration. "Golf is a puzzle without an answer. It's an extremely sad game, a frustrating game in which you can see your greatest shots end in disaster. Golf, to be sure, is too tough to solve."

Golf is a cruel sport and an increasingly popular sport, too—especially in North America, Europe, Australia, and the Orient.

But while golf can be an alternately likable and loathsome game, it is definitely a source of cultural psychosis: more and more earthlings are crazy about the game. According to the National Golf Foundation in Jupiter, Florida, the book-keepers of the sport, 24.7 million people play golf in North America; another 32,750,573 people play the game outside North America.

In Japan, golf balls can cost $5 apiece, golf shirts can cost $100, greens fees, meals, and transportation at public courses can cost $240 per round, and private club memberships can cost $1 million, but there is no shortage of money or golfers there. What the country lacks is facilities. There are just 1,500 golf courses to accommodate nearly 15 million golfers. So these days, in order to

JAPAN GOLF

■

Capitalism and golf are playing partners in Japan, where the demand for course time substantially exceeds the supply of courses in the country. Private club memberships are often sold or bought at extravagant prices, as though they were precious shares of stock in some extraordinarily successful company. Indeed, profiteers sometimes purchase memberships from the Tokyo Stock Exchange as speculative investments.

In 1987, a Japanese golfer offered a record $3.57 million for a membership at the exclusive Koganei Country Club, but the proposition was rejected. Memberships apparently are priceless keepsakes in Japan.

Opposite page: Golf is an unpredictable sport— it sometimes takes golfers one, two, three, four, or more shots to put the ball this close to the hole. Above right: Golfers need more than a yen to play the sport in Japan; they usually need several thousand yen or more to gain access to courses there.

reduce the long waiting lines at courses and to add facilities, the Land of the Rising Sun apparently is becoming the Land of the Falling Mountain.

"The Japanese," American golf course architect Bob van Hagge says, "blow up mountaintops, then say: 'Okay, architect, come here. Design and build us a golf course.'"

In Russia, citizens will soon be experiencing *parestroika*. Robert Trent Jones's championship course in an exquisite forest outside of Moscow, the first golf course in the country, will open in the early nineties.

Chess is the national pastime of the country, but then–Soviet President Mikhail Gorbachev evidently recognized more big business is completed on golf courses than across chessboards. "The Soviet government is very serious about this," Jones said. "It's important to them economically and politically. They want to open up to a sport that's played by business people and diplomats around the world. The Soviet Union is the last major nation that does not play golf."

The golf season near Moscow will be shorter than normal—from May through September— but daily playing times will be considerably longer than any place in North America, because the sun shines from four A.M. until eleven P.M. that far north.

Earth has become a planet of golfers, it seems. Cindy Cooper, a club pro from New Jersey, says she arrives at work at six A.M. some weekdays and immediately asks herself: "So, does anybody work anymore?" The receiving line of sixty to sixty-five cars in the parking area is what prompts her concern and altogether reasonable inquiry.

"There are days," Cooper says, "when all of the tee times, twelve hours of tee times, are gone by seven A.M." Golfers' morning priorities these days appear to be a tee time, then that first cup of coffee.

According to NGF estimates, there were 7.5 million more golfers in the United States in 1989 than there were in 1985. Golf soon may be the most popular form of outdoor recreation in the country. "It's like a disease," says Jim Esposito of New Jersey, a typical weekend golfer. "I played off and on when I was younger and started up again regularly ten years ago."

There is more evidence than one golfing revivalist and heavy traffic at public courses across the country that the United States is a nation of golf junkies.

Dave Nelson, another public course professional from New Jersey, pauses one Saturday morning at 8:35 A.M. to answer the telephone and a frequent question: "What tee time is available?" When Nelson tells the caller, "Three-twenty P.M.," the reply is loud and typical: "You've got to be kidding."

"There are so many golfers and just so many golf courses to accommodate them," says Nelson, whose public course regularly accommodates 292 players Saturdays and Sundays during the golf season, but turns away dozens more, a common occurrence at other public golf courses as well.

What impulse compels countless weekend golfers to rise along with the sun from roughly the beginning of April until the end of November? "It's a sickness…a nice sickness," Jim Esposito says. "We'd play even earlier if they'd let us. I wish we could start every day like this." Esposito, and his regular partners, Joe Elsman and Emery Depuis, awaken at 5:15 A.M. every Saturday morning during the golf season, ensuring them enough time to shower, shave, dress, eat, and reach their favorite course by 6:15 A.M., tee-minus forty-five minutes.

Esposito, Elsman, and Depuis are good friends and earnest, typical golfers—have been since 1983, will be indefinitely. The three are golf addicts and husbands of golf widows.

Golfers, historically, have been incapable of controlling their habit. Golf was so popular in the 1400s that King James II of Scotland had to outlaw the game because the frivolous national pastime was greatly interfering with national security. Scots of all kinds, it seems, were practicing golf more than archery—thus improving their games but weakening the defense of the country. So on May 16, 1491, James II announced to Parliament in Edinburgh: "It is statute an ordinit that in no place of the realme be there usit…golfe or uther sik unprofitabill sportis."

Clubs and balls can be munitions in the hands of bad golfers, so a battle between an

Gene Littler: *"Golf is not a game of great shots. It's a game of the most accurate misses. The people who win make the smallest mistakes."*

DEFINITIONS

Birdie: One stroke below the designated par of a hole. Derivation unknown.

Eagle: Two strokes below the designated par of a hole. Derivation unknown.

Bogey: One stroke more than the designated par of a hole. In Great Britain, bogey is the number of strokes that the average golfer should make on a hole (on some easier holes, par and bogey may be the same). Its negative connotation apparently derives from an English poem from the 1890s:

Hush! Hush! Hush!

Here comes the bogey man!

So, hide your head, beneath the clothes,

He'll catch you if he can!

"Bogey" supposedly became synonymous with golfing calamity at the Great Yarmouth Club, when Major Charles Wellman told Dr. Thomas Browne during one of their friendly matches:

"This course of yours is a real bogeyman!"

Opposite page: The roots of golf, according to the most reliable evidence available, sprouted in Scotland in the 1400s. But the Dutch claim to be its originators, too. Above right: Golfers, from the beginning, have been people full of excuses, luck, theories, and hope.

© Allsport

ancient foursome of barbarous, scattershot golfers and a brigade of warriors armed with bows and arrows probably would have been quite sporting, maybe even unfair. James II would not have agreed with that supposition, but no matter. In 1502, King James IV was seen playing the game, and golf was back on course in its home country.

Mary Queen of Scots was one of the original golf junkies. Several days after the murder of her husband, Lord Darnley, she was supposedly observed playing golf "pall mall in the fields beside Seton." Insensitivity was one of the charges at her subsequent trial. Mary eventually lost the case and her head in 1587. The judge, jury, and executioner evidently were unaware that golf causes much more grief than it relieves.

Golf still can be a humbling and vexing game. A sense of humor and two or three dozen balls per season are golfing imperatives.

"I *cahn't* play as *bahdly* as I did on the first nine," Eric Collins says in proper English while standing on the tenth tee at Sunset Valley Golf Course in New Jersey.

His wistful plea is wishful thinking. His drive

fades right, right into a grove of trees.

Golfers are full of excuses, theories, and hope. "Hmmm. Maybe if I try a different-color ball..." says Chris Casey, addressing both an orange ball and his partners one Saturday. The experiment is successful. This time. A perfectly struck tee shot lands in the middle of the tenth fairway at Sunset Valley.

In the life of every golfer there are embarrassing moments—like when the divot flies farther than his or her golf ball. In the life of every golfer, there also are exhilarating experiences—like when his or her golf ball obliges the golfer and actually follows the correct trajectory and flight path, and lands in the cup.

Andy Volcz was such an astonished golfer one day at Sunset Valley. His second shot at Number 9, a par-4, knew its place—the bottom of the cup. In the time it took the ball to fly 190 yards, land, then roll 10 yards into the hole, Volcz had made an "eagle. An eagle."

A shot such as Volcz's is what makes golf such a seductive and attractive game to millions and millions of earthlings.

The Players

The life of professional golfers looks easy from behind the rope separating the sports world from the everyday world. But not every member of the three major Professional Golfers Association tours—PGA, LPGA, PGA Senior—earns fat paychecks, eats caviar, and sips gin-and-tonics on the verandas of lush country clubs.

A pro's swing appears as effortless to spectators as the life-style itself, but playing for a living is work.

Chuuunk!…Grrrr.…Thwack!…Ahhhh. Those are the common sounds of golfers at work on the practice tee, a laboratory of sorts where men and women pros experiment with their swings, committing perfect results to muscle memory.

Pro golfers always seem to lead perfect lives. They work outdoors and have suntans that even lifeguards envy. Their offices are emerald green courses, instead of windowless cubicles beside the water cooler or the bathroom.

Pros play four days, and the winner usually receives a check worth the same amount of money ordinary folks earn every five years.

The best professional golfers have the same earning potential as the smartest investment bankers, but golfers are different from other professional athletes, because there are no guaranteed contracts on any of the tours. How well the golfer performs determines the size of his or her weekly paycheck. The total can be enviable one week and negligible the following week.

The tours do not supply team planes or meal money, either.

What follows next are the stories of eighteen of the finest golfers in history, champions all.

Sevé Ballesteros

SEVERIANO BALLESTEROS HAS charisma, an expressive face TV cameras love, and all the shots. Off the tee, he belts a golf ball mightily, yet sometimes waywardly. His bravery, strength, and imagination made him one of the youngest golfers in history to win two major championships (he won the Masters and British Open before turning twenty-four), and the youngest Masters titlist in history.

Ballesteros was born in Pedrena, Spain, with the perfect golf swing. His aggressive approach to the game is the same as Arnold Palmer and Greg Norman's. He is similar to Palmer and Norman, too, because sometimes he has trouble easing his foot from the accelerator. He knows only one way to attack golf courses: at stampede speed. Ballesteros has won two Masters titles (1980 and 1983) and three British Open championships (1979, 1984, and 1988), using his giddyap style and greatest gift, his resourcefulness.

He has lost tournaments with the same stubborn style, too. Ballesteros was tracking the Masters title in 1986 and 1987, but made untimely bogeys in the fourth round of each tournament and lost more than money and the championships; Ballesteros temporarily lost his confidence, an almighty golfing commodity.

New York, not Scotland, England, or Spain, was where he found both his lost confidence and putting stroke in June 1988. In order to find him before the fourth round of one of the myriad Corporate-Advertising-Classics on the regular tour, one had to search the bunkers, woods, and middle of the field. Ballesteros was there most of the time during the first three rounds at Westchester Country Club. In the end, though, there was Ballesteros atop the leader board having beaten Norman, David Frost, and Ken Green on the first hole of their play-off.

The victory was Ballesteros's first in America since 1985, but afterward he was talking more about a serious loss—the loss of his putting touch following the 1987 Masters. He was third in that tournament, but had the chance to finish first before bogeying the first hole of a play-off with Norman and the champion that year, Larry Mize.

Opposite page: Sevé Ballesteros does not play golf courses—he attacks them. Above: On the course, Ballesteros is alternately stubborn, stylish, remorseless, and resourceful.

Ballesteros won the Westchester Classic at Number 10. He was in the best position of the foursome off the tee, and his ball was lying on the downslope of the front bunker approximately seventy-five feet from the hole. His stance was awkward—he had to balance himself with his right foot extending outside the trap—but his shot was practically perfect.

The ball landed four feet from the cup and victory.

Ballesteros's ability to escape from traps, woods, and rough has made him one of the most popular professional golfers on Earth, and among the wealthiest, too. He won the British Open in 1988 at Royal Lytham St. Annes with one more incredible shot at the sixteenth hole. Ballesteros was wearing the same blue sweater and trousers

he wore in 1979, when he won his first British Open. He was sharing first place with Nick Price of South Africa, but in the time it took his golf ball to fly some 100 yards, Ballesteros was three inches from one more birdie and his third British Open title. "He hit a perfect wedge," Price said. Ballesteros, who needed just sixty-five strokes to defeat Price and the course, thought the shot was the best and most important of his career.

According to his standards, Ballesteros has been slumping since then.

"When I play good, any green is good for me usually," he says. "When I play bad, nothing is good."

The remarks sum up streaky Sevé Ballesteros, who plays golf with the bravado of a matador, and often is as daring as he is unpredictable.

JoAnne Carner

JOANNE CARNER SPENT ABOUT THIRTEEN years of her LPGA career traveling inside a motor home, touring America on a virtually perpetual, and tremendously successful, business trip. She accumulated unbelievable amounts of mileage along the way and also the sort of souvenirs unavailable in gift shops anywhere: victories galore, more than $2.3 million in prize money through 1990, and recognition as one of the finest professional golfers of all time, woman or man.

"I've had a good career. I have a good record," she says.

"Great" aptly describes her achievements, including being the second woman to earn both $1 million and $2 million, and induction into the LPGA Hall of Fame in 1982 and the World Golf Hall of Fame in 1985. But good, period, is how Carner reacts to success. Her nonchalance belies her accomplishments.

"I wish I'd been a little more consistent, or done better in the major championships," she says.

All Carner did in the majors was finish first in two U.S. Open championships in the 1970s, and finish second a total of nine times in the Open, du Maurier Classic, Dinah Shore, and LPGA Championship during the 1970s and 1980s.

One word explains her unwillingness to enthusiastically acknowledge her position in golf history. "Greedy," she says, laughing. She has won more tournaments than all but six golfers in LPGA history, but not enough to satisfy herself. Carner has the same attitude as the LPGA pioneers: Victories impress her more than paychecks. If she were a man, people would call her a good ol' boy. To Carner, *life* is another word for fun.

Golf was a sport to attempt and master when she was growing up in Kirkland, Washington. In 1956, at the age of seventeen, she won her first U.S. Amateur title. The experience was so exhilarating that she continued her amateur career and won four more U.S. Amateurs between 1960 and 1968. Her five titles overall is a record.

The pro tour life-style did not seduce or interest Carner until 1969, when she won the Burndine's Invitational.

"I really had no desire to turn pro earlier than thirty," she says. "Then I decided, what more can I do as an amateur, besides repeating as champion at tournaments? The next step up was to test myself against pros."

Distinction as the last amateur to win an LPGA tournament was as useless to Carner as her clubs in 1970, her first year in the golf business. She figures there were essentially five women capable of consistently winning tournaments when she began her pro career. But Carner was not among them, originally.

"I shot more eighties than anybody, though."

The line pleases her. She laughs and begins to recount her first frustrating season on the tour. She won one tournament in 1970, but too little success exasperated Carner, the most dominant amateur female golfer since Babe Zaharias.

"I found out in 1973 you had to have a good teacher, what pros call a 'pro's pro.' I had kind of outgrown the local pro at home."

Carner began working with Gardner Dickinson, who won seven tournaments on the PGA Tour in the 1950s, 1960s, and early 1970s, and is known as one of the best golf instructors in America. He must be good because, Carner says, "In three lessons Gardner transformed me from just another professional golfer to the leading money winner."

Indeed, in 1974, Carner led the LPGA with earnings of $87,094, and was among the top ten money winners until 1985, when she finished eleventh.

Rearming her with new clubs was the important part of the Dickinson battle plan. Carner remembers, "I hit shots with each one of my old clubs, and, one by one, Gardner took the clubs from me and threw them out." New clubs were weapons in her hands, and with them and her rebuilt swing, she won forty-two tournaments through 1990.

There is more to Carner than victories. She has charisma and power. Aside from being one of the finest golfers around, she remains one of the longest drivers in LPGA history (typically, she drives between 250 and 260 yards)—and not in terms of annual mileage, either. "I've never had a classic swing," she says, pausing before following through strongly. "My philosophy always has been, fire and fall back. Most golfers are afraid to make bogeys, but when I make one, I figure I just have to make more birdies."

JoAnne Carner is a golfer who is as confident as she is durable.

"I used to have a friend who told me to be prepared to retire at thirty-five. When I was playing well at thirty-five, she told me to prepare to retire at forty. When I was the leading money winner at the age of forty-four, she shut up."

Carner is past fifty now, and she and her husband, Don, spend less time reading road signs inside their motor home and spend more time observing the ocean view from inside their Palm Beach, Florida, condominium.

The victory tour of America completed, JoAnne Carner can finally relax more, fish with Don on their boat, and admire her souvenirs.

Opposite page: JoAnne Carter credits, among others, Sam Snead and Gardner Dickinson for creating the powerful swing that has made her one of the greatest golfers in LPGA history. Below: Carter was one of the best amateur golfers in America, but did not succeed immediately as a pro. She eventually won the LPGA Player of the Year award three times.

© Bob Thomas Sports Photography

© Simon Bruty/Allsport

Above: Nick Faldo was alone atop the subjective list of Best Golfers in the World in 1990, the year he won his second Masters and British Open titles. Opposite page: Faldo was ''unfulfilled and confused'' in major championships until he won the 1987 British Open title with his rebuilt swing.

Nick Faldo

"FOLDO" WAS HOW THE EUROPEAN press knew Nick Faldo of England before he won four major championships in three years. "Foldo" was his uncomplimentary nickname because his game and nerves were known to unravel in the final rounds of major tournaments.

Faldo lost his cruel nickname when he won the 1987 British Open at Muirfield with eighteen pars in the fourth round, then won consecutive Masters titles in 1989 and 1990 and another British Open championship at St. Andrews in 1990.

The consecutive Masters victories alone are proof of his ability to withstand immeasurable pressure. Jack Nicklaus, after all, is the only other golfer in history to leave Augusta National Golf Club wearing the garish but prestigious green jacket two years in succession.

Some people were nominating Faldo for the subjective title of Best Golfer in the World in 1990 because of his recent record in the majors.

Hale Irwin was one of them. His opinion was significant, because in 1990, at the age of forty-five, Irwin won his third U.S. Open title. He says, "Nick's performances in the majors over the past few years have shown there is no other contender for the title."

Faldo may not be the indisputable ringmaster of the "Greatest Show on Turf," but he unquestionably was one of the dominant male golfers on Earth the last two years of the 1980s and at the beginning of the 1990s.

Require more evidence than the scorecard? Is Nicklaus's official endorsement enough? "When you get to that next level, as Curtis (Strange) has, as Nick has, you must rebalance your life, find a new pace. That doesn't mean changing your intensity or concentration. It means dealing with that new status, and I think Faldo will," says Nicklaus

Will success warp Faldo, the phlegmatic par machine? Not likely. He seemingly plays golf and lives life in the same trance Bjorn Borg was in when Borg won Wimbledon five consecutive years. But Faldo, it turns out, is not impervious to pressure or oblivious to his achievement.

"Majors drain you," he says. "You run on an adrenaline high for the full week until, win or lose, you have nothing left in you. But who cares? I give it what I've got, then recover. I remember going out to play the Tuesday after the (1990) Masters, and I got to the second hole and asked my caddie how she felt. She was afraid to tell me, but then I told her just how much of a basket case I was. But that's why they're called majors, right?"

Faldo rebuilt his career and swing with help from golf teacher David Leadbetter, beginning in 1984. He had won plenty of regular tournaments on the European Tour with his old swing, but in the major worldwide tournaments Faldo was nothing more than a dejected contender.

He described his frustration in the introduction of Leadbetter's book, *The Golf Swing*.

He wrote: "I had won five tournaments on the way to topping the Order of Merit in 1983. I had contended in more than one major championship before falling away over the final nine holes. Enough for some people, perhaps, but I was unfulfilled…and confused."

Faldo met Leadbetter near the end of 1984, but did not commit to reconstructing his swing until May 1985. Professional golfers are protective of their clubs and their swings, and changing either, or both, is an important life decision. You get the feeling that professional golfers are sometimes more attached to their swings and clubs than to their spouses. It's not a fact, just a hunch.

Leadbetter told Faldo that altering and perfecting his swing would require two years of work. Leadbetter is known to be a good teacher, and apparently is a wonderful prognosticator. Two years and two months later, Faldo won the 1987 British Open title.

"He's done something that's awfully courageous," says Curtis Strange, who defeated Faldo in a play-off for the 1988 U.S. Open championship. He changed his whole swing in midstream. I can identify with that to a point, because I did, too, sacrificing distance for accuracy after I got out of college. But that's it. I was a lot younger. He did it after enjoying some success. He'd already won, and he didn't win again until 1987, and during that time he didn't know whether he'd ever win again, didn't know whether the new way would work. That takes some backbone."

What Faldo did exactly to his swing was widen its base, flatten its arc, and reduce the number of moving parts. Good golf is as much work and repetition as fun, so Faldo spent hours a day at the practice tee, the place where the swings, games, and confidence of champions are built.

"Silver trophies are more important than paperwork," he says. "I don't think about whether I'm the best player in the game, because that can be a week-to-week judgment. But if my swing remains intact, I think I can compete at the top level the remainder of the decade. And when it's over for me, I'd like to be remembered as someone who could really play the game."

In 1990, Faldo was the best golfer on the planet, but he is not yet the world dominator. "Domination is winning six or seven major championships over four or five years," says Nicklaus, winner of eighteen major professional titles, the most in golf history. "How many has Faldo won? Four? He will have to win a few more before you can start talking about dominating the game."

Domination aside, Nick Faldo and his rebuilt swing are constructing an impressive record together.

© Rogers/Bob Thomas Sports Photography

GOLF BALL

■

Rocks, eggs, nuggets, and pellets are the pseudonyms for golf balls—the seemingly witless spheres that sometimes are actually more obedient than house pets.

"Down, down," golfers plead. "Sit, sit," golfers command.

Often the ball hears the appeal, complies, and sometimes even performs an extra trick—it rolls backward. Golf balls actually go forward and in reverse, but only experts know how to consistently engage the second gear.

There are times when angry golfers scold the ball, and its revenge is to travel in the wrong direction or to stop rolling too soon when approaching the cup.

Creating a sturdier, controllable, obliging golf ball has been the project of golf enthusiasts since the inception of the game.

In the early seventeenth century, golf balls were misshapen leather pouches full of goose feathers. "Featheries" flew tremendous distances but had major shortcomings besides their severe expense: They were fragile and devoid of durability.

"Gutties" were the successor to featheries. Gutties were golf balls handmade from *gutta-percha*, a gum extract from Malaysia. Gutties were smooth as billiard balls until the 1870s, when some perceptive golfers noticed the ball flew longer and truer with nicks on its exterior.

Gutties were the first revolutionary advance in the long history of the sport, because they were much cheaper than featheries, perfectly round, and practically indestructible.

In 1902, the modern golf ball was born, adding about twenty yards to drives. It was made in three pieces, with a rubber core around which hundreds of yards of thin rubber thread was wound. The core of that ball then was encased in gutta-percha.

Aside from the aerodynamic advancement of inverted dimples, improvements to the coverings (balata or Surlyn; tough, strong plastics), and variations on the substance of the core (hard rubber or wound liquid centers), the type of ball Greg Norman or Jack Nicklaus or Nancy Lopez slug nowadays is not so different from the ball Harry Vardon, Willie Anderson, and Laurie Auchterlonie were belting up or down fairways at the beginning of the twentieth century.

All golf ball manufacturers these days brag that their product flies farther and lands softer, deliberately ignoring the fact that their aircraft of sorts is only as good as the pilot steering it.

What advantage is the "longest ball," if all it does is fly farther into the woods?

What imaginative golf ball manufacturers ought to produce is an aromatic ball, one expert caddies or bloodhounds can track and find in a forest or tall rough.

Courtesy Titleist Golf Division

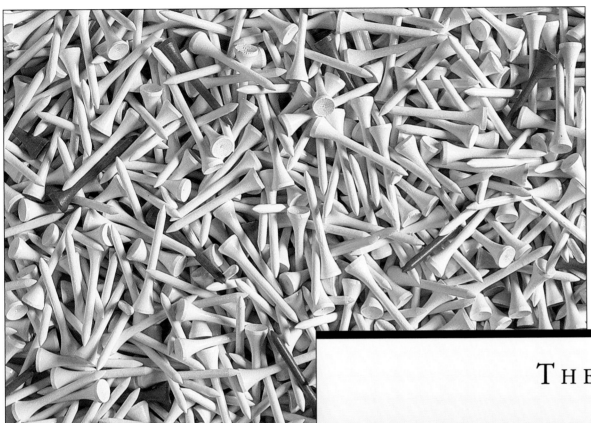

© Christopher Bain

Opposite page: Golf balls are such inviting targets. So how can such stationary prey so often torment and confound its smarter, but hapless, hunter? Left: Traditional tees can be temporary sources of confidence to trembling golfers.

© Sam C. Pierson Jr.

THE TEE

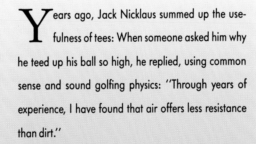

Years ago, Jack Nicklaus summed up the usefulness of tees: When someone asked him why he teed up his ball so high, he replied, using common sense and sound golfing physics: "Through years of experience, I have found that air offers less resistance than dirt."

Tees are launching pads of a sort and an inspiration to average golfers who derive some confidence from seeing their golf ball in the air...until, of course, it is struck incorrectly and rolls pitifully one hundred yards or less down the fairway.

The traditional "arrow" wooden tee, a painted peg usually made from either birch or maple, is a young innovation in an old game—gaining universal acceptance and use only in the 1940s, some five centuries after the origination of the sport.

In the past, when golf was known as gawf or golfe, it was the caddies' job to carry, besides a bagful of clubs, a bucket of sand and a mold. The caddie used the sand and mold to form a tee, in actuality a dirt pile, for his golfer at each new hole.

William Lowell, a dentist from Maplewood, New Jersey, was the inventor of the standard tee. Lowell, apparently thinking sand would irritate his hands—office equipment as vital and precious to him as any drill—developed the first wooden tee in 1922.

Tees, besides elevating the ball and confidence level of golfers, have one more use: Tees dutifully absorb stress from furious golfers, who, following another poor shot, regularly swing their clubs like sledgehammers, burying an old tee further into the turf with the impact.

Walter Hagen

U NTIL WALTER HAGEN CAME ALONG, professional golfers were more unpopular at country clubs than increases in dues and membership fees. When Hagen began his career, amateurs were gentlemen and pros were rogues. But then "The Haig" gave pros legitimacy and publicity.

He was the Great Gatsby of golf, the perfect Roaring Twenties golfer: sumptuous, pompous, and carefree. His background was blue collar, but he wore silk shirts, silk ties, blazing argyles, crisp trousers, alpaca sweaters, saddle shoes, and gold cuff links to work. There was enough oil on his hair to lubricate six automobile transmissions. He ate vichyssoise, roast duck, and drank champagne at lunch, then went out and often won another tournament or exhibition match.

Hagen was one of the first athletes to earn more than $1 million, but since he spent money as though he had $2 or $3 million, he was often broke. The $23,000 he made on an exhibition tour of the world in the mid 1920s somehow did not cover all his travel expenses. When he arrived in the United States, he had to remain in his hotel room in San Francisco three days because he did not have enough cash to pay the hotel launderer and retrieve his clothes.

Figuring out Hagen was no easier than defeating him. He was intensely competitive one day and just as indifferent on other occasions. He grew up wanting to pitch in the major leagues, and reluctantly made his living on golf courses instead.

In the first round of the 1920 British Open he shot 37 going out, 48 coming in, and 85 overall. Hagen, of course, did better in the second round—but not much better. He shot 84 and eventually wound up in fifty-fifth place, playing each shot in the fourth round as though he were closer to first than to last.

"I was scared I might finish fifty-sixth," he told a newspaperman who asked Hagen why he had been so deliberate.

When Hagen was serious, instead of frivolous, he was one of the great golfers of his era. He won eleven major championships (five PGA

© Paul Thompson/FPG International

Championships, four British Opens, and two U.S. Opens), a record until Jack Nicklaus won his twelfth two generations later.

He was the master of match play (competition by holes instead of strokes), the PGA Championship format from 1916 until 1958. Hagen was a despicable and estimable gamesman, and match play was the perfect format for him to use his powers of psychology, because match play is such a personal competition between golfers.

Hagen would often discourage his opponents by wandering over to their bags uninvited, inspecting their clubs, shaking his head sorrowfully, then returning confidently to his own bag, with his supposedly superior collection of clubs. He won four consecutive PGA Championships using those kind of tactics, and more than sixty international tournaments.

For nine years in succession, he played an average of 125 exhibitions, in addition to his regular schedule of tournaments. His imitation aristocracy and peculiar charm won him countless dollars and won acceptance for pros across the country and around the world.

Opposite page: Walter Hagen was a swaggering, swanky golfer from the Golden Age of professional golf. Below: Hagen, standing behind Henry Cotton, was an excellent player and an intimidating gamesman.

Ben Hogan, *on putting: "Selecting a stroke is like selecting a wife. To each his own."*

Above: Proud, pugnacious Ben Hogan is one of six golfers in history to win two successive U.S. Open titles. Opposite page: Success was sometimes difficult to attain, but Hogan wound up being one of the best golfers of all time anyway. In his career, Hogan was able to mesmerize galleries, even in 1970, at the age of fifty-eight.

Ben Hogan

GOLF WAS MORE THAN THE WAY BEN Hogan made his living. Golf was his compulsion. His form was classical, faultless. The game he played was easy only in spectators' eyes, though. He understood the physics of golf better than anyone, because he practiced more than anyone.

To consult with Hogan was to sit at the feet of the master and to gain enlightenment…or at least advice on how to approach the thirteenth green at Augusta National without sacrificing another ball to the golfing demons lurking in Rae's Creek.

Hogan. He needs no other identification.

When someone grumbles about the severity of the slopes on Masters greens, tournament chairman Hord Hardin replies gruffly, "Hogan would find a way."

Hogan. The name is another word meaning "winner."

Hogan was alternately proud and pugnacious during his career. Gray, dour, and unapproachable describe him, too. His remoteness often was the result of his desire and need to play golf in a trance. He outshot so many opponents because he outthought so many opponents.

He first was attracted to the game by the wages he could earn caddying as a child—sixty-five cents a loop. Golf gradually became his inamorata. He grew to love the game more than anyone before him, and he became one of the special golfers in history.

"You play a game with which I am unfamiliar," Bobby Jones told Hogan years before he repeated the compliment to Jack Nicklaus.

He drove himself and his golf balls continually in order to be the best, though success was difficult to achieve. Hogan was thirty-four years old before he won his first major championship, the same age Palmer was when he won his seventh. Hogan was thirty-six before he finally won the U.S. Open in 1948.

He had to wait until 1950 to try again, because he almost lost his life in a car accident. He was driving at dawn on Highway 80 between Fort Worth and Van Horn, Texas. Visibility was poor because of dense fog. Hogan did not see the speeding bus heading toward him until the two vehicles met.

Hogan sacrificed his body to save the life of his wife, Valerie. The first fear was that he would not live. The second fear was that he would not walk. He pushed himself to recover from injuries to his pelvis, a shoulder, a rib, and an ankle.

Hogan had to somehow rebuild his body and swing. He had to recall his greatness. He shot 69 in the second, third, and fourth rounds of the 1950 Los Angeles Open, shared first with Sam Snead, but lost to him in a play-off. Defeat did not matter, because the tournament was a test of his strength, not his golfing ability, which was already a recognized fact.

The final 200 yards he negotiated famously, memorably, with a one iron at Merion in the 1950 U.S. Open. The approach shot on the seventy-second hole put him in a play-off against Lloyd Mangrum and George Fazio.

He shot 69 and won the play-off and his second open. He won his third open in 1951, and fourth in 1953, the year he won the Masters again, and also the British Open at Carnoustie. In all, Hogan won nine major championships and sixty-two tournaments.

The most moving Masters moment came on April 8, 1967, the day Hogan, four months short of turning fifty-five, took everyone in the gallery with him on a farewell tour of Augusta National Golf Club. He shot 30 on the back nine and 66 overall, the lowest score of the tournament.

Hogan.

Every golfer recognizes his name, even those who never saw him play.

© Sam C. Pierson Jr.

Brunskill/Bob Thomas Sports Photography

GOLF FASHION

■

When it comes to fashion, most golfers have their own personal style. Who else wears plaids and stripes together without embarrassment? Or an ensemble of fluorescent yellow pants, a violet shirt, and chartreuse shoes? Remember, too, golfers popularized lime green pants with navy blue whales or navy blue sailboats on them.

Golfers were stylish in the past, when Ben Hogan, Byron Nelson, and Sam Snead were identifiable because of their caps and hats as much as for their talent.

Okay, Payne Stewart wears knickers these days, but only because it is his gimmick, not because he is making a fashion statement.

The menagerie of knit shirts with tigers, penguins, and alligators on them is the fault of clothing manufacturers hoping to appeal to and please golfers—the weekend and professional varieties. And golfers wear such outfits in order to emulate their heroes, and pros can earn bundles of money endorsing lines of golf wear, clubs, balls, shoes, and gloves.

Left: *His radiant shirts, sweaters, socks, and trademark knickers serve as Payne Stewart's ID on the golf course. Opposite page: Ben Hogan's attire, including his signature cap, was as simple and elegant as his game.*

Bobby Jones*: "Competitive golf is played mainly on a five-and-a-half-inch course, the one between your ears."*

Bobby Jones

BOBBY JONES UNDERSTOOD MORE THAN the mechanics of golf, he also understood the mystery and misery of the game.

"On the golf course," he once wrote, "a man may be the dogged victim of inexorable fate, be st. uck down by an appalling stroke of tragedy, become the hero of unbelievable melodrama, or the clown in a side-splitting comedy—any of these within a few hours, and all without having to bury a corpse or repair a tangled personality."

Jones philosophized about the game as well as he played it, and he was the best golfer of his time. He was an amateur his entire career and essentially a weekend golfer, but he won thirteen national titles in eight years, four of them in 1930.

His swing was as economical as it was flawless, and his game was so balanced that experts disagreed on the best part. He did not pound practice balls until his hands bled. Golf was so instinctive to him, it is difficult to believe he dreamed about being a professional baseball player, but he did.

His short career was like a squarely struck drive, the kind Greg Norman launches daily during the golf season. The kind that begins at eye level, rises, soars, then lands on the fairway 300 yards or more from the tee box.

Jones's prime was brief—eight years. He was not a golfer in the sense that he played tournament after tournament to sharpen his swing and game. Jones was a champion. His record in national championships was incredible from 1922 through 1929—in seventeen national championships he finished either first or second all but four times.

Then in 1930 he accomplished the improbable, what golf experts thought was impossible. Jones won the Grand Slam—the U.S. and British opens and the U.S. and British Amateur championships. Privately, Jones always thought the feat was possible. Scottish golfer Bobby Cruickshank predicted the performance when Jones won the

© FPG International

1930 Southeastern Open in Augusta, Georgia, by thirteen strokes!

"They'll never stop him this year," Cruickshank told O.B. Keeler, Jones's confidant.

Jones nearly did not win the Grand Slam because he almost lost the British Amateur, the first major championship of his remarkable run, during his match against Cyril Tolley, the defending champion. In match play, golfers compete by holes instead of strokes. The winner of the first hole is said to be one up. A golfer increases his lead every time he wins another hole. A match ends when one player is more holes up than there are holes remaining to play.

Jones's match against Tolley was even on the eighteenth hole, but Tolley was twelve feet from

victory. He missed the birdie putt, and Jones won at the first extra hole. He was two down with five holes remaining in his fifth match, but won two up. The final was easy: He won seven and six, against Roger Wethered, on the thirtieth hole.

Jones was uncharacteristically sloppy during the British Open, but his total of 291 broke the course record at Holyoke by ten strokes anyway. He won the third leg of the Slam by becoming the first man in U.S. Open history to break par for seventy-two holes.

At the U.S. Amateur, Jones was the medalist, shooting 69 and 73 at Merion in the two qualifying rounds. He eventually won the tournament and the Slam, eight and seven, against Gene Homans.

Bobby Jones was the best golfer of his time, winning thirteen national titles in eight years, including a Grand Slam in 1930.

Jones gave up the game at the age of twenty-eight, surrendering to unmatchable success and the pressure of being "Unbeatable" Bobby Jones.

His uncharacteristically vague acceptance speech during the U.S. Amateur trophy ceremony doubled as his farewell address to championship golf: "I expect to play golf," he said, "but just when and where, I cannot say now."

Jones beat the pros at their own game, but he never did join them; although he did renounce his amateur status in order to accept the endorsement offers filling his Atlanta law office.

After his retirement, Jones designed clubs and constructed the Augusta National Golf Club with Alistair McKenzie. His legacy to the game was his impressive record and the Masters.

Above: Nancy Lopez is considered the Jack Nicklaus of the LPGA Tour because she is both marketable and promotable. She also is similar to Sam Snead, because, like him, the U.S. Open trophy is missing from her mantel. Opposite page: In her second season on the LPGA Tour, Lopez won a record five consecutive tournaments. Her rewards were almost $189,000 in prize money and designation as Rookie of the Year.

Nancy Lopez

FOLLOW THE LONGEST UNBROKEN TRAIL of spectators at an LPGA tournament, the one made up of hundreds and hundreds of people stretching from the tee box to the green, and usually at the end of it is Nancy Lopez. Lopez is the Jack Nicklaus of the LPGA Tour. She is the number one attraction on the Ladies' Tour, and one of the most popular professional golfers of all time because of her exceptional ability and obliging personality. She cannot pose for every picture or scribble her signature on every program thrust into her hands, but her rooters understand. There is no griping; her presence normally is enough to satisfy them.

The members of the LPGA galleries treat Lopez as a close friend rather than just one more sports dignitary. Indeed, Lopez, Nicklaus, Arnold Palmer, and Lee Trevino form a golfing Mount Rushmore of sorts because of their rare combination of skill and charisma.

"Nancy" is how Lopez's rooters identify her. Spectators at tournaments she enters invariably wonder aloud: "Where's Nancy's group?"

In explaining Lopez's sweeping popularity, golf observers point first to her personality, then to the fact that aside from glamorous, flamboyant Jan Stephenson, no other woman golfer has been able to capture the attention of the golfing public. There are dozens of terrific women golfers in the world. But how many can anyone name? How many can anyone instantly recognize?

Pat Bradley, not Lopez, is the leading money winner in LPGA history, accumulating more than $3.3 million in prize money. Bradley and Betsy King have won more major LPGA Championships than Lopez, and Patty Sheehan has won the same number as Lopez—three. But none of them can match or overshadow Lopez's appeal. She enjoys the attention, but Lopez wishes more people would notice and appreciate the achievements of her colleagues. "For some reason," she says, "no one wants to give them credit for playing well."

Lopez was consistently sensational in the early years of her LPGA career, which began in 1977. In her second season, Lopez won nine tournaments, five of them in succession. In 1979, she won eight more tournaments, and by 1987, at the age of thirty, she was the eleventh member of the LPGA Hall of Fame.

"From eight feet in, she is the best [putter] man, woman, or child," says Curtis Strange.

Lopez, who won forty-three tournaments and more than $3 million through 1990, is only a part-time golfer these days, but remains the main draw, anyway. She cannot, and does not, devote all of her time to maintaining or improving her golf game anymore. Her daughters, Ashley and Erinn, and her husband, former major-leaguer Ray Knight, mean much more to her than another title, another trophy, or another paycheck.

"There're days when I think my family has suffered," she says, "and there are days when I know my golf has suffered. I don't like finishing thirtieth or fortieth, but when I do, I know the reason. My family. These days, because of Ashley, Erinn, and Ray, I have to settle for playing poorly or playing well, but just missing out on another victory. When I'm not at the top of my game it's because I'm cheating [on practice time]."

All this does not mean Lopez has given up entirely on being the best. "If I go an entire day without practicing," she says, "I don't feel good. I feel guilty. But I always feel guilty if I don't do something with every aspect of my life. Once in a while, I'll think: Golly, I could be home with my family and be a bit more normal. But winning is such a fun thing."

The one souvenir missing from her career is a U.S. Open championship. She has come close to winning the title twice, once as an amateur in 1975.

"I feel pretty good about my life and what I've accomplished," she says. "I realize you can't be 'Super Mom.' It's impossible. All you can do is be your best when you're with your children, with your husband, and when you're on the tour."

Byron Nelson

A RANCH IN ROANOKE, TEXAS, IS A monument to the one golf record more remarkable than all the others. When Nelson won eleven consecutive PGA tournaments in 1945, he was not attempting to construct an almighty, unbreakable record, he was merely attempting to build his dream home. The weekly prize money was an incentive and also the down payment on the spread he lives on to this day.

Nelson says, "The joke among all the guys then was 'Nelson's saving to buy the darn ranch one cow and one acre at a time.'"

Nelson is full of golf history and golf stories he remembers well, because he repeats them so often.

He grew up in the 1920s and 1930s idolizing the flamboyant Walter Hagen, who kept on swinging even after he left the eighteenth hole. Right here Nelson rewinds to a memory about the time he and Hagen were partners more than fifty years ago, in the fourth round of the General Brock Open at Niagara Falls, New York.

Nelson had Hagen and the rest of the field right where he wanted them: behind him. The first three rounds of the tournament, though, were a false start. The tournament truly began in the fourth round. See, Nelson found out that playing alongside Hagen was more difficult than needing to sink a twenty-five-foot putt to defeat him.

He remembers stammering when learning the pairings. In those days Nelson was unknown, and meeting Hagen was unsettling. Hagen was known to be an unscrupulous gamesman, especially against winless, anxious golfers greener than putting surfaces.

When it was tee time, Nelson was nervous, and Hagen was late. Purposely late. Putt, chip, and fuss was what Nelson did until, about two hours later, Hagen came strolling up to the first tee. He was typically remote.

"Hi, kid," he told Nelson.

"It's…it's…an honor," Nelson told Hagen, becoming the first person to speak while in a coma.

Nelson lost his composure and his aim on the front nine. He shot 42 going out, 35 coming

in, and wound up in second place. Nelson won $600, which was not enough money to retire on, but was enough money to fret about losing.

"Louise," Nelson recalls telling his wife, "we've got to hide all this money before we start out toward the next tournament. We're wealthy now, we're bound to get robbed. If we hide the money, maybe the thieves won't get it."

The PGA Tour was a roving circus of sorts when Nelson began his career in the 1930s. The Greatest Show on Turf went from town to town across America in a caravan of cars. Flying from site to site was possible then, but too expensive.

"[Ben] Hogan, [Jimmy] Demaret, [Craig] Wood, [Vic] Ghezzi, [Horton] Smith, [Gene] Sarazen, [Sam] Snead, we'd follow each other from tournament to tournament," Nelson says.

In between 1944 and 1945, and along the the PGA trail, Nelson thought about the short-comings in his estimable game. He kept notations about every tournament in a diary, and from studying the entries saw dumb errors were preventing him from winning more tournaments.

"I always had one careless chip, one careless putt per round," he says. "I made up my mind to reduce the number of careless shots to zero."

He did become more careful than careless, because in 1945 Nelson won nineteen tourna-ments, eleven of them in succession, both unap-proachable PGA records. The victory tour of North America began in Miami on March 8 and continued through the Canadian Open on August 4. Nelson actually won a twelfth consecutive tour-nament in Spring Lake, New Jersey, but the event was unofficial because the prize money of $2,500 was $500 too small to meet PGA standards. The remarkable run ended when he finished fourth in the Memphis Invitational, a tournament won by amateur Fred Haas.

"Staying hot was easy," he says, "because I wasn't interrupted by TV or commercial offers. I did only one commercial during the period, for Wheaties, and that was only worth two hundred dollars."

Nelson probably thought he had won the lottery without buying a ticket. His take was $30,250, good money then, but hardly a jackpot. The same feat today would be worth about $2 million in prize money and countless dollars in endorsement fees.

His scoring average during the run (67.47) was as amazing as the binge itself.

In all, Nelson won fifty-four tournaments in his career, including five major championships. He left golf in 1946 to return to his ranch. In his lifetime, Byron Nelson has been a golfer, rancher, broadcaster, course designer, and foremost an unmatchable winner.

Opposite page: Byron Nelson built his dream house with help from an impeccable swing and a remarkable run of winning golf. Below: Nelson had an extraordinary impact on both the history of the game and his protégé, Tom Watson (right).

© David Cannon/Allsport

GOLF CLUB

■

Golf clubs once were crooked hickory sticks with character and peculiar nicknames: spoon, cleek, mashie, niblick, mashie-niblick. Golf clubs nowadays are "cavity-backed," "perimeter-weighted," "investment-cast," "internal-strut," "inertial" promises made from graphite or forged carbon steel or beryllium or titanium or metal alloys, and hyperbole, plenty of hyperbole.

Manufacturers of clubs embellish the effectiveness and features of their products, essentially guaranteeing acquisitive golfers looking to purchase a better game, greater distance, uncanny accuracy, and "sweet spots" wider than some fairways.

Some of the space-age advancements do improve the game of many golfers, and one in particular, "square grooves," was the cause of controversy and two lawsuits in 1990.

On one side was Karsten Solheim, tinkerer extraordinaire and manufacturer of Ping Eye-2 clubs, the most popular irons in the royal and ancient history of golf.

On the opposite side of the issue, having filed separate suits, were the Royal and Ancient Golf Club of St. Andrews, the USGA, and the PGA Tour.

Separating the sides was two-thousandths of an inch, the microscopic space between grooves on the club face of Ping irons.

The spacing seems insignificant, but the R and A and USGA are extremely protective of tradition. The USGA approves of some flexibility in the shafts of clubs, but virtually none in the ineffaceable general rules of the sport.

Square grooves essentially act as brakes, theoretically enabling shots to stop faster on greens, even shots from ugly rough, by catching more grass, absorbing more moisture, and producing a spin rate nearly twenty revolutions more per second than conventional clubs.

In 1987, the USGA first told Solheim that the distance between grooves on Ping irons was much too close to meet its exact specifications.

Solheim disputed the measuring mechanism, the findings, too, and originally sought more than one club's length relief in court. He sought a total of $100 million from the R and A and USGA before settling the matter out of court.

Solheim, an old aircraft engineer, agreed to both recognize the USGA as the governing body of golf and to manufacture in the future grooves that conform to USGA standards. The USGA agreed to declare older Ping irons legal.

A circuit court of appeals in America had yet to decide *Solheim* v. *PGA Tour* at the time of this writing.

Square grooves were seen by many older PGA Tour golfers as one more invader on the tradition of the game and were opposed with the same vehemence that rubber-cored golf balls and steel shafts had been in the past.

Tom Watson thought the clubs evened the sides unfairly between the "talented and the not so talented."

Jack Nicklaus said the advancement was making it more difficult "for the cream to rise to the top."

Tom Kite thought all pros ought to return to the auld days, because "if you played with really primitive clubs, the best player would have an even better chance of winning."

Professional golfers accept change readily, but only from the cashier working at the pro shop.

Courtesy Spalding Sports Worldwide

Tommy "Thunder" Bolt is a testy, touchy, cranky, cross golfer who has flung almost as many clubs as he has swung.

"If you are going to throw a club," he once said, "it is important to throw it ahead of you, so you don't waste energy going back to pick it up."

Courtesy Wilson Sporting Goods

Courtesy Titleist Golf Division

Manufacturers often exaggerate the effectiveness of their clubs—enticing golfers of varying skill to purchase their products. But some modern improvements actually fulfill their promises—woods made of metal (above) are one of them. Putters (far left) are professional golfers' money machines. "Drive for show and putt for dough" is an old adage. The slogan on these Titleist irons (left) sure sounds authoritative and persuasive, so what desperate golfer could ignore it?

© Michael Tenney/Transparencies, Inc.

Jack Nicklaus

THE CYCLE OF SPORTS PRODUCES FEW geniuses—someone whom crowds adore and opponents admire, envy, and chase for ten, fifteen, twenty years, maybe longer. Jack Nicklaus is a golfing genius in the tradition of Harry Vardon, Walter Hagen, Bobby Jones, Gene Sarazen, Sam Snead, Ben Hogan, Arnold Palmer, Gary Player, Tom Watson, and…?

Golfing geniuses in the world today are rarer than double eagles.

"People say how much better younger golfers are nowadays," says Player, part of "the Triumvirate" of professional golf with Nicklaus and Arnold Palmer in the 1960s. "Hogwash, I say. Jack Nicklaus is so much better than any younger player today. I can't think about any of them being better than Jack Nicklaus, and I've played with them all."

Jack William Nicklaus is about monotonous consistency and excellence, not the kind of ersatz excellence owners of sports teams reward so generously and frequently nowadays. He is not the best driver, short-iron player, or long-iron player of all time. Nicklaus is not the finest putter in the history of golf, though he seems to sink all the important putts. He is simply, unarguably, pro golf's greatest champion.

His grip and swing were considered unusual in 1959, when he was an overweight amateur from Columbus, Ohio. He won two U.S. Amateur titles, but no one knew Nicklaus was going to be one of the exceptional golfers someday, except "the King"—Arnold Palmer, not Elvis Presley.

"Wait 'til you see this kid from Ohio," Palmer announced then. "He can beat anybody."

The kid from Ohio did not win all the time, but believing himself unbeatable did intimidate some opponents and help Nicklaus build his record and reputation.

"When you go head to head against Nicklaus," J.C. Snead says, "he knows he's going to beat you, you know he's going to beat you, and he knows you know he's going to beat you."

Singling out one or two of Nicklaus's accomplishments is difficult, because there have been so many since 1961. In his PGA and Senior

Tour careers, Nicklaus has won seventy-two tournaments overall, including eighteen major championships (six Masters titles, five PGA championships, four U.S. Opens, and three British Opens). He has won more major titles than anyone, compiling a record that is quite possibly unapproachable, probably unmatchable, and very likely unbreakable. "Someday someone will come along who is six-foot-six, can drive the par-fours, has a great touch around the greens, and has both the dedication and the desire—he'll surpass my records. All I can do is to make those records as difficult to beat as I can. But they'll be beaten. Sometime. By somebody…I can't make them impossible to break."

The golfer capable of surpassing Nicklaus's marks may be learning the game on some public course somewhere on the planet. He does not appear to be on tour.

Pro golfers these days are more intent on making money than on making history. Earnings from tournaments and side businesses in golf course design, construction, and management, plus publishing, promotion, and sportswear, have made Nicklaus oil-sheik rich. Accumulating bales of cash never was his objective, though. His goal was to amass the most major titles in history—to him, and to others, the caliper with which to best measure the greatness of a professional golfer.

Not only has Nicklaus won seven more major tournaments than Walter Hagen, nine more than Gary Player and Ben Hogan, eleven more than Sam Snead, Arnold Palmer, and Gene Sarazen; he has won more major titles than Hogan and Snead put together, more than Palmer and Player put together, and more than Lee Trevino and Tom Watson put together.

When winning regular tournaments was neither challenging nor stimulating anymore, winning major championships became Nicklaus's priority beginning in 1969. Nicklaus's attainment of his goal is a tribute to his uncommon determination and his orderly plan.

"There was nothing for me to prove in the week-to-week tournaments. I couldn't get up, get excited, for the routine tournaments. I found myself going through the motions. You can't play golf that way."

Reducing his schedule to about twelve tournaments annually and pointing toward the major

© Bob Thomas Sports Photography

Opposite page: *The Golden Bear, Jack Nicklaus, is a rare animal in professional golf. He cares more about history and victories than cash.* **Above:** *Nicklaus set his mind on winning more major championships than any golfer before him and achieved his goal, a tribute to both his talent and determination.*

© David Cannon/Allsport

tournaments regenerated Nicklaus's enthusiasm.

"I like golf. I like the competition. And on the schedule I was on, I was nearing the end of my career prematurely. So I cut back."

Before reducing his schedule, he won twenty-seven PGA events, among them three Masters, two U.S. Opens, and one PGA Championship, also one British Open title and two Australian Opens, and was Player of the Year from 1962 to 1968. Beginning in 1969 and ending in 1986, Nicklaus won forty-four PGA events, four Player of the Year awards, three Tournament Players Championships, four Australian Opens, and eleven major championships: three Masters, four PGAs, two U.S. Opens, and two British Opens.

Nicklaus's victory in the 1986 Masters, at the age of forty-six, should have been the quintessential finale to his career—akin to Ted Williams belting a home run in his final at bat with the Boston Red Sox. The tears teeming from his eyes as he was walking up the fairway at Number 18 were enough to swell the banks of Rae's Creek, the despicable water hole that yearly drowns the hopes of all but one golfer bent on beating Augusta National Golf Club. He had sunk the last three of his birdie putts at Number 17 to win the Masters—a record sixth time. Nicklaus had not won a tournament since May 1984, but suddenly, unexpectedly, his golf ball knew its place—the bottom of the cup.

"That was pretty special, probably the most special of them all," he said.

His 65 in the final round was not some quirky, nostalgic burst, a sentimental surge of adrenaline. His 65 was some of that old Jack magic.

"What Jack did at Augusta was the best thing to ever happen to golf," said Lee Trevino. "It's more of an achievement than [jockey] Willie Shoemaker winning the Kentucky Derby [at the age of 54], because you've got to remember one thing: Willie Shoemaker didn't carry his horse across the finish line."

Nicklaus has been playing the back nine of his career since 1980, the year he won the U.S. Open, then the PGA Championship by a record margin. Nicklaus, though, is as competitive in his fifties as he was in his twenties, thirties, or forties.

"It's human nature to enjoy making money. Making money, and only making money, is satisfying—except for people who want to be the best in their sport. You've got to have the desire to win, to keep working at it," he says.

He still needs the kind of competition only the regular tour can provide him, so retiring to the Senior Tour and competing against men his age and older does not yet interest Nicklaus.

"My days as the best player in the world are over, I know that. My problem is that I like to play golf. I suppose I'll play more senior golf…when I get it into my head that I can't compete anymore on the regular tour. I don't have that in my head yet."

Jack William Nicklaus has another goal, one more goal: to become the first golfer to win a Senior Tour and PGA Tour event in the same season.

Opposite page: Course and conditions were immaterial obstacles to success for Jack Nicklaus, arguably the finest golfer in the history of the game. Below: Nicklaus may be the most complete golfer of all time. He was the PGA Player of the Year in 1967, '72, '73, '75, and '76; has been a member of the World Golf Hall of Fame since 1974; and was named Golfer of the Century in 1988.

Greg Norman

GREG NORMAN PLAYS GOLF WITH THE commando mentality of a middle line-backer. He attacks courses worldwide headfirst, full speed ahead.

Norman grew up in Australia idolizing Jack Nicklaus, yet he favors the swashbuckling, charging style of Arnold Palmer. His adventurous attitude and uncommon aptitude for the game have made Norman one of the most popular professional male golfers in the United States, Europe, Australia, and Asia.

Norman, though, may end up being one of those luckless athletes people remember more for the way he lost than for the way he won, even if he has won more than $4 million in prize money and more than sixty international tournaments from Hong Kong to Hilton Head.

Victories nowadays at regular tournaments make professional golfers rich. But victories at major tournaments make professional golfers immortal and elevate them atop the mantel of special golfers alongside Vardon, Hagen, Jones, Snead, Hogan, Nicklaus, Palmer, Player, and Watson. Norman has the jutting confidence of those champions. What he craves now is their success and acclaim.

"I've been so close," he says. "When you get close, it whets your appetite. You want to go out and win as many as possible."

The "Great White Shark" has hooked six major championships, but has landed only one of them since joining the PGA Tour in 1983 at the age of twenty-eight. He has lost play-offs in the British Open, the U.S. Open, and the Masters. He has lost on the seventy-second hole at Augusta once and once on the seventy-second hole in the PGA Championship.

The professional Grand Slam and Norman were playing partners in 1986. He led all four major championships at the end of fifty-four holes that year, a first. He won just one of those tournaments, the British Open at Turnberry.

Nicklaus shot 30 on the back nine at Augusta, 65 overall, and overtook Norman and Tom Kite in the fourth round of the Masters. In the fourth round of the U.S. Open at Shinnecock

Hills, Norman shot 75 and fell from from first to sharing twelfth. He lost all four shots of his lead in the final round of the 1986 PGA Championship at Inverness, near Toledo, Ohio. Then he lost the tournament on the last hole, when Bob Tway, with whom he was sharing first place, sank a blast from a bunker so deep, Tway barely was able to see the top of the flag, let alone the top of the leader board.

In the British Open, Norman fought Turnberry to a stand-off. But even par 280 was the winning score, his lucky number.

Norman, and the world, thought he was going to win the Masters play-off in 1987 before Larry Mize somehow sank "The Shot," a miracle chip that flew ninety feet…bounced on the eleventh green once, twice…then rolled fifty feet into the cup and golf history.

"Sometimes you play bad golf and win. Sometimes you play great golf and lose," Norman says philosophically, nearly poetically. "That's golf. That's history. It's done. It's behind me."

His most painful defeat was at the 1989 British Open at Royal Troon. He began the final round closer to last than to first. But Norman birdied the first six holes, lipped out a birdie putt at Number 7, and ended up shooting a 64 and sharing first place with Mark Calcavecchia and compatriot Wayne Grady.

He led the sudden-death play-off by two strokes until the fourth and last hole, when he launched his tee shot 325 yards into a fairway trap that was supposedly unreachable, even by a pro as strong as Norman.

When Calcavecchia hit his second shot stiff, Norman thought he had to be bold and went for the green. The ball kissed the lip of the first trap and popped into another trap. The ball went out of bounds on his third shot. Norman dejectedly picked up the ball and stowed it in his pocket, essentially conceding defeat and the hole to Calcavecchia, who sank his birdie putt.

"People said afterward I shouldn't have hit a driver. But if I'd hit it three yards to the left, those people would have been saying I hit the greatest drive ever."

Critics call Norman reckless. He prefers fearless. Reckless, fearless, whatever—Greg Norman definitely is an uncommon golfer. He is rakishly handsome, with a surfer's tan, a muscular build,

and hair the color of spotless beach sand. But while Norman is blond, he is not one of the pack of mechanical blonds on tour, all of whom hit long drives nearly every green and are content to finish anywhere from fifth to tenth on the prize-money list.

Norman has the carefree, roguish disposition of an old-time riverboat gambler. When he plays golf, he always goes for broke in hopes of winning every pot.

Norman often energizes his game and the gallery in the third and fourth rounds of tournaments with improbable comebacks.

"I can't answer why I shoot those scores. Maybe it's the challenge. Maybe it's payday."

He expects to win every tournament he enters. The public expects the same result. Greg Norman has even more potential than confidence, so someday he may satisfy the critics, the public, and himself.

© David Cannon/Allsport

Opposite page: Greg Norman idolizes Jack Nicklaus, but emulates Arnold Palmer. Norman, like Palmer, does not retreat from challenges or hazards, and sometimes his fearlessness costs him money and victories. Above: Norman did not take up golf until he was sixteen years old. He learned the game, he says, by reading two of Nicklaus's books—Golf My Way and 55 Ways to Play Golf.

© Barry Rabinowitz/FPG International

Above: Arnold Palmer charges each golf course as though he were an angry caveman with a club. He is not smooth or graceful—just successful. Opposite page: His daring, fearless style has made Palmer rich and famous. He was the first player in PGA history to earn more than $1 million in prize money. The top money winner on the PGA Tour now receives the "Arnold Palmer Award."

Arnold Palmer

WE KNOW HIM BEST BY HIS NICK-NAME, his stage name: Arnie. Our favorite sports heroes need no more than one name. Arnold Palmer is the identity Arnie uses in formal United States Golf Association commercials, in the record books, or when endorsing paychecks.

But Arnie is how his enormous army addresses its commander. Informality and vitality, Arnie gave both to golf in 1960. He did not, repeat, did not invent the game, although it seems he deserves almost as much credit as the ancient Scots for its origination.

What Arnie did do was to perfect professional golf, transforming a small business into a corporation by hitching up his pants and being himself. Courageous. Bold. Telegenic. Palmer gave professional golf popularity, personality, and, foremost, television appeal.

Professional golfers earn Wall Street wages these days because Arnie made golf likable beyond private country clubs. His charisma gave golf more than galleries; his charisma gave golf an audience, in this instance the world. "He's the king; everyone knows it," Canadian golfer Dave Barr says. "He may not be the best golfer in the world, but he brought golf to where it is today."

In his prime, Palmer would test himself and the diabolical course every round. Ponds, sand traps, and rough were not obstacles, but challenges.

"There's something about him," American golfer Mark Calcavecchia says. "When he walks by, he's still Arnold Palmer."

Finishing second, fifth, eighth, ninth, any of the careful positions on the leader board, did not interest Palmer when he was younger. First was his objective. Always.

Absolute proof of his purpose is visible at the first tee of Cherry Hills Country Club in Denver, Colorado. A plaque there commemorates one of the most astounding and famous tee shots in golf history—Arnie's first shot in the final round of the 1960 U.S. Open.

When the round began, Palmer was trailing fourteen golfers. He was seven shots behind the leader, Mike Souchak. Retreating was an unpardonable option, he thought. Attack the field and the course. The beachhead was hole Number 1, 346 yards from tee to green.

Placement was thought to be more important than power there. Palmer, though, unsheathed his driver, his weapon of choice on the first hole in the previous three rounds, when he had made six, five, and four, respectively.

Special golfers like Palmer expect to make three on such short holes. In this instance, though, Arnie was thinking eagle, not birdie. He drew back his driver and in no time the speeding club head struck the face of the stationary golf ball squarely and with the identical impact an oncoming wrecking ball makes against the side of a dilapidated building. Whack!

Palmer does not rhythmically sweep a golf ball from the tee or ground—never has, never will. He lashes violently at the ball with the same chopping motion lumberjacks use to fell an ancient redwood with an ax.

The force he created with his swing was powerful enough to launch his golf ball 340 yards, and also launch an entire era. The nature of the tournament, and of professional golf for that matter, changed with that one exceptional drive.

"It was the 'sweetness' of the risk that I remember, and not its dangers," he wrote of the experience in his autobiography.

Palmer did not sink the eagle putt, but three was an acceptable score, because the birdie triggered one of the most explosive stretches of golf in history. He chipped in for a birdie at Number 2, and made another birdie at Number 3. He birdied Number 4 by sinking a snaking forty-foot putt. A par at Number 5 interrupted the birdie binge, but Palmer made up more ground with birdies at Number 6 and Number 7. He went out in thirty and was angry he did not shoot twenty-nine.

Palmer and Souchak were tied by the tenth hole. Palmer was ahead by the twelfth hole. By the eighteenth, he overtook the fourteen golfers ahead of him. Palmer wound up shooting 65 in the final round, and 280 for the championship. His boldness was the difference in the tournament. But then, daring defines his career and distinguishes it from the careers of other golfers.

He always went for broke and ended up rich. Palmer does not earn his living anymore solely by playing golf. Arnie is a conglomerate. Prize money is not the only means of supporting oneself in professional golf. He reportedly earns more than $8 million annually—the most money made by any professional athlete apart from heavyweight boxers—from endorsement and commercial fees, real estate development, car dealerships, course design, and construction.

People willingly pay him lumps of cash because people worldwide revere Palmer. He no longer has a championship game, only a championship aura.

People enlisted in his army in 1960 because of the way he won. Passionately and powerfully. Grumbling and grinning. Charging to the ball and to victory after another remarkable shot, usually on Sunday of some tournament.

Defeats affected his army more than victories. When he lost, Arnie's army was crestfallen. His pain was their pain. His greatest satisfaction was winning the 1960 U.S. Open. His greatest disappointment was losing the 1966 U.S. Open at the Olympic Club in San Francisco, California. Palmer was ahead of his partner, Billy Casper, by seven shots with nine holes to play. A gimme, agreed? Well, Arnie lost his concentration, his aggressiveness, and all of his lead, too. Eventually he lost the tournament to Casper in a play-off.

"I forgot what my pop taught me years ago," Palmer says. "He told me always to be a gentleman on the golf course, but if I ever get an opponent down, don't let him up."

In all, Arnie won sixty-one tournaments in twenty-six years on the PGA Tour. He won all the major championships, except the PGA. He gained a negative fame for coming close three times.

The Senior Tour, where he has won ten tournaments since 1981, has become more than a retirement village for older golfers because of Arnie and his aging army.

Palmer is more than sixty years old, but his competitiveness and loyalty to his army continue to drive him. "I'm always aware that [the army] is there," he says. "I hope they know that."

Palmer is different from professional golfers of today, who, it seems, talk openly only with their valets, wives, secretaries, agents, managers, copilots, or caddies. Palmer is always himself, and because of his earnestness, Palmer always will be Arnie to his army and the rest of the world.

Arnold Palmer: *"What other people may find in poetry or art museums, I find in the flight of a good drive—the white ball sailing up into the blue sky, growing smaller and smaller, then suddenly reaching its apex… curving, falling, and finally dropping to the turf to roll some more, just the way I planned it."*

© Stephen Wade/Allsport

Gary Player

Gary Player: "There is absolutely nothing humorous at the Masters. Here, small dogs do not bark and babies do not cry."

GARY PLAYER HAS BEEN WALKING purposely up fairways since 1950, always looking as though he is heading somewhere farther, indeed somewhere other, than just the next green.

It's true Player has built his ample reputation and substantial fortune on hundreds and hundreds of golf courses worldwide, but golf is merely his livelihood, not his entire life.

"Golf is one of the best lessons in life," he says, temporarily reverting to his first job in the sport, that of a teaching professional. "Golf teaches you respect. Golf teaches you to be humble. Actually, it forces you to be humble. Golf teaches you to be patient. Golf has a certain set of rules, and I believe life needs a certain set of rules, too."

Player somehow turns typical sports speak into philosophy with his colorful and logical approach to life. He never has been one of the nameless, faceless, or indifferent golfers of the present—many of whom have blond hair, blue eyes, and Pepsodent smiles, equate second place with victory, mistake comfort for success, and rarely seem willing to converse about anything more substantial than techniques of proper course management and positive swing thoughts.

Player's bottomless supplies of energy, opinions, and confidence are what make him one of the special golfers. His favorite anecdote demonstrates how much he trusts both himself and his golfing ability.

In 1954, when he was an assistant at Virginia Park Country Club in his hometown of Johannesburg, South Africa, Player says a wealthy South African man made him an incredible investment proposal.

Player was nineteen years old and earning fifty cents a lesson teaching golf, but the man was offering him a lifetime contract and a guaranteed fortune. His autograph at the bottom of a contract was worth R500,000—then the equivalent of about $2 million—to the man who was going to bankroll Player's career in return for half of Player's winnings for the remainder of Player's professional life. But even then Player had the swing,

© Bob Thomas Sports Photography

bravery, and determination of a champion: "No" was his reply to the man.

"The man told me to show the contract to my father," Player says. "My father was a coal miner who worked twelve to fifteen thousand feet underground and never made more than two hundred fifty dollars a month in his life; he didn't know anything about contracts. I was earning only thirty dollars a month at the time, but I had enough confidence in myself to reject the offer. Money isn't the thing that drives champions."

Player did not begin playing golf until he was fifteen years old, but his dedication to fitness and the game has made him one of the most prolific golfers of all time.

He has won twenty-one PGA Tour tournaments, sixteen Senior Tour titles, and nine major championships, the same number as Ben Hogan, and the third-highest total in professional golfing history. Player is one of only four golfers to have won, at least once, all four majors: the Masters, the British Open, the U.S. Open, and the PGA Championship. Gene Sarazen, Nicklaus, and Hogan are the others.

His mantel is full of trophies won at tournaments held from Augusta to Australia. Player has more than 130 international titles to his credit, and also a place in the World Golf Hall of Fame.

He was the first truly global golfer. Player figures he has flown more miles than any athlete. He probably has accumulated more air mileage than many commercial pilots.

His longevity and success are the results of talent and daily exercise. Player probably spends as many hours in a gym working out every week as he spends at the practice range working on his estimable golf game. "Rest means rust," he says.

His age qualifies him as a senior golfer—but his body is as sturdy as it was twenty-five or thirty years ago, when Player was one of the "Big Three" of golf with the legendary Arnold Palmer and Jack Nicklaus.

He rides a stationary bike thirty-five minutes a day, lifts weights for twenty-five minutes, does 100 to 300 sit-ups, and practice swings with a weighted club in order to strengthen his body and satisfy his competitive cravings. "I've always worked hard," he says. "It's part of my system to do things that keep me young. If you sit down, you're finished."

Player has been an able champion for more than four decades because he drives more than a golf ball. He incessantly drives himself, too. That's always been his style.

He made up seven shots on the leader, Hubie Green, in the final round of the 1978 Masters by making birdies on seven of the last ten holes. He shot sixty-four that day, won the tournament by a stroke, and added a third green jacket to his collection.

The following week at the Tournament of Champions he was trailing Sevé Ballesteros by seven shots through three rounds. He wound up winning the title by two strokes. Seven days later, Player became the Houston Open champion, and the last PGA player to win three consecutive tournaments.

All those improbable results help summarize Player, who has more money and fame than he needs, but continually pushes himself, anyway.

Gary Player is fifty-seven years old, looks forty-seven, and acts even younger. He proves golfers are ageless athletes.

He still competes on the Senior Tour when he is not supervising the construction of another golf course somewhere on the planet. In 1990, he personally oversaw the completion of forty-three golf courses.

His golfing accomplishments have made Player famous in his home country and around the world, but his anti-apartheid posture has also made him notorious with some South Africans, particularly radical conservatives.

"Yes, some of my countrymen do consider me a traitor," he says proudly. "I was brought up correctly. You've got to do the Christian thing."

Injustice, especially in his homeland, is one topic Player often addresses, usually as frequently as he addresses another golf shot. He employs scores of otherwise unemployable black citizens

on his ranch in Johannesburg, and more than 300 children receive an education inside the school he built on the grounds. It delights Player to help his compatriots and witness the gradual downfall of apartheid.

"Gary is someone in whom I can trust," says Lee Elder, one of the first truly successful and accepted black golfers in America and a close friend and colleague of Player's since 1967.

"I like him so much because, like me, he's always said and done what's in his heart rather than what other people expected him to say or do."

Professional athletes nowadays generally promote themselves instead of issues. Player is atypical of his peers, and all the necessary proof can be found in his vigorous walk and passionate words.

GOLF GLOVE

■

Outfielders, infielders, catchers, and pitchers were the only professional athletes who wore work gloves every day before the 1940s, the decade when Sam Snead began donning one regularly on golf courses worldwide.

Golf gloves were available in England as early as the beginning of the twentieth century, but were obscure aids, and did not become truly popular equipment until the 1950s.

Snead, a marvelous professional golfer and an amateur philosopher, once told reporters: "If a lot of people gripped a knife and fork like they do a golf club, they'd starve to death."

The point of the remark was to emphasize the importance of the hands and grip in an effective, repetitive golf swing. Cashing in on two golfing imperatives apparently was the intent of profiteers masquerading as gadgeteers in 1966, the year Rod Campbell, a driving-range professional from Pennsylvania, and Dr. Stanley K. Herberts, an optometrist from Philadelphia, designed a golf glove guaranteed to provide extra distance to its wearer.

What Campbell and Herberts did was insert four ounces of buckshot into the glove. The additional weight in the back of the glove supposedly made the hands accelerate through the ball faster, and more club-head speed means farther shots, as many as seventy-five extra yards, according to the designers.

What the two did was actually ingenious, but illegal according to the rigid rule makers of golf.

Gloves that conform to USGA standards provide a surer grip on the club, so nowadays gloveless golfers—professionals, amateurs, and hackers—are rarer than bogeyless rounds.

Center: Gloves serve two important purposes: They help golfers hold their weapon of choice, and they conceal fingerprints in the event an angry golfer wants to strangle the grip, or even drown an unobliging club in a water hole. Opposite page: Writing about golf is easier than mastering the sport— a hunch is all it takes, but one supportable by the plethora of golf literature in stores, on bookshelves, and in libraries worldwide.

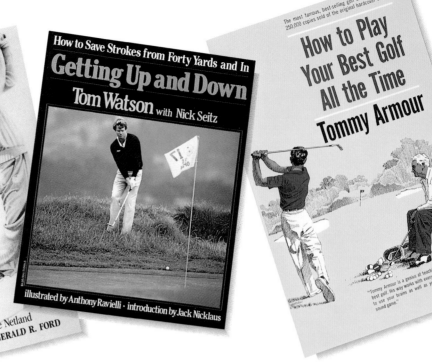

Courtesy Foot-Joy, Inc.

FIVE BEST INSTRUCTION BOOKS

(IN ALPHABETICAL ORDER)

1. *Five Lessons*, by Ben Hogan with Herbert Warren Wind (Fireside, 1957)

2. *Getting Up and Down*, by Tom Watson with Nick Seitz (Vintage, 1983)

3. *How to Play Your Best Golf All the Time*, by Tommy Armour (Simon and Schuster, 1953)

4. *Play Better Golf*, vols. I and II, by Jack Nicklaus (Pocket Books, 1980, 1981)

5. *Play Great Golf*, by Arnold Palmer (Doubleday, 1987)

FIVE MOST ENTERTAINING GOLF BOOKS

(IN ALPHABETICAL ORDER)

1. *The Bogey Man*, by George Plimpton (Harper & Row, 1967)

2. *Confessions of a Hooker*, by Bob Hope as told to Dwayne Netland (Doubleday, 1987)

3. *Dead Solid Perfect*, by Dan Jenkins (Price Stern Sloan, 1986)

4. *The Snake in the Sand Trap*, by Lee Trevino and Sam Blair (Henry Holt, 1985)

5. *Strokes of Genius*, by Thomas Boswell (Doubleday, 1986)

Gene Sarazen

THE SECOND SHOT GENE SARAZEN struck at the fifteenth hole of Augusta National fifty-seven years ago submerged into the hole, but has yet to stop rolling. Sarazen has gotten incredible mileage from a shot he launched some 240 yards into the cup in the fourth round of the 1935 Masters. He continues to talk about the double eagle, though reluctantly.

"It was a lucky shot," he says. "It meant so much at the time, but, you know, I get tired of hearing about it."

The Shot, he says, is about all he remembers nowadays from an exceptional golf career that began in the 1920s.

"You'd think I'd never done anything else but hit that shot," he says. "I've met about twenty thousand people who claim to have seen it."

None of them was under oath at the time, though. The shot was no more believable than the "witnesses" themselves.

Sarazen was three shots behind Craig Wood, who was in the clubhouse contemplating, and actually celebrating, his victory. The odds did not favor a Sarazen win, but what was he supposed to do? March off the course into the clubhouse and announce: "I surrender."

In order just to match Wood's 282 total, Sarazen would somehow have to manage three birdies on the final four holes. The chances were better of April snow showers in Georgia covering the azaleas, magnolias, dogwood, and junipers at the Cathedral in the Pines.

He struck his tee shot at Number 15 and was in the middle of the fairway calculating the remaining distance to the hole, along with the probability of catching Wood. He was not thinking about making two on the hole, Sarazen remembers. He was hoping to make four on the par-5. His playing partner, flamboyant Walter Hagen, was hoping to make it to dinner on time. "Hey, please hurry up, Gene," Hagen told Sarazen. "I've got a date tonight." Sarazen ignored Hagen's plea and also advice from his caddie. His caddie said: "You've got to hit a three-wood if you want to clear that water."

Instead, Sarazen unsheathed his four-wood. Hagen disagreed with the club selection.

"Well, that's that," he muttered to Sarazen.

"Oh, I don't know, they might go in from anywhere," Sarazen told Hagen, though with how much confidence only he knew.

The ball landed on the green, and eventually in the cup. Sarazen was calm afterwards, or perhaps numb.

He says, "The first thing I thought was what I would have to do to tie Wood. I felt no elation. It happened so quickly."

The double eagle alone did not do in Wood; Sarazen had to par Numbers 16, 17, and 18, then defeat Wood in a thirty-six-hole play-off.

During his career, Sarazen invented the sand wedge, won the U.S. Open at the age of twenty, won thirty-eight titles overall, seven major championships, and was the first golfer to win the Masters, U.S. Open, British Open, and PGA Championship at least once.

No matter. The Shot in the second Masters is Sarazen's legacy to golf. Bobby Jones and Alister McKenzie built the Augusta National Golf Club, but it was Sarazen who made the Masters famous and prestigious with his stroke of luck, his stroke of genius.

Opposite page: Gene Sarazen, ''Squire'' to his peers, seldom found himself in such predicaments. He is one of the original Golfing Gods and Golfing Geniuses.

© Wide World Photos

Sam Snead*: "The only reason I played golf was so I could afford to go hunting and fishing."*

Sam Snead

SAM SNEAD IS PLAIN FOLK FROM Virginia, who grew up playing barefoot and hustling ten dollars or more from any sucker who mistook him for a hillbilly.

Golf came easy to "Slammin' Sammy," except when he was seven years old. When Snead was a youngster, he would struggle while caddying at the Homestead in Hot Springs, Virginia, a resort course up a piece from his house, as Southerners would say.

"The bags got so big, it got to the point where you had to weigh eighty pounds to carry them," Snead says.

He learned all the aspects of golf at the Homestead, including his sweet swing. Snead, the assistant pro at the age of twenty-three, had one of his first encounters with the best professional golfers at the Homestead in 1935.

He was the hometown hero, but also the least-known golfer in the Cascades Open field that year. The field was trailing him, though, until he lost some of his aim, concentration, confidence, nerve, grip, and a golf ball on one of the holes on the back nine.

"I was playing with my boss, and he started needling me," Snead says. "He said, 'How can you expect to be a great golfer if you hold your left elbow like that?'

"I tucked it in and the ball went way into the woods. I made an eight on the hole. But he was right, I did have to change my grip. I held the club too tight. I was driving with a three-wood because I couldn't lift the ball off the ground with a driver."

Snead corrected the flaw in his grip, learned to hit with the driver and all of the other clubs in his bag, and went on to win more golf tournaments than any man in history.

He won his first tournament in 1936 and wound up his PGA career with more than one hundred victories, eighty-one in official tournaments.

Experts argue that Bobby Jones and Ben Hogan were better golfers, but Snead was more colorful and charismatic than either of them. Had television been available everywhere when Snead

was in his prime, he, not Arnold Palmer, would have brought golf to the masses. He came from a period in golf history when players had talent and personalities, when golfers were emotional and entertaining, and unafraid to rattle and throw clubs, or kibitz with the gallery. "You can't do that now," he says. "I like characters. I like that [Craig] Stadler; you watch him after he hits a bad shot, and he wants to bury that club."

The size of purses inhibits pros nowadays. Money talks—but few players do on the course. Lapses in concentration may cost them thousands of dollars, they reason. Golf is more popular than ever, but somehow not as amusing as it was when Snead was playing full-time.

He and Boston Red Sox left fielder Ted Williams, a Hall of Famer and arguably the finest hitter of all time, would feud amiably in the newspapers about the difficulty of their respective sports. Williams would declare there was nothing

harder than slugging a baseball, and Snead would crack, "In golf, we have to play our foul balls."

He was one of the greatest golfers in history —his opinion along with other's. His record and trophy case are incomplete, though, because he never won the U.S. Open.

Victories in three Masters (1949, 1952, 1954), one British Open (1946), and three PGA Championships (1942, 1949, 1952) never did offset his one failure.

He is a remarkable golfer, anyway, because of his achievements and longevity. He holds plenty of PGA records, among them most victories in one event (eight) and oldest winner. In 1965, he was fifty-two years and ten months old when he won his eighth Greensboro Open title.

Sam Snead does not see well anymore, and he cannot finish eighteen holes without a cart, but he still can shoot his age or lower and still swings effortlessly, gracefully, and sweetly.

Opposite page: *His sweet swing made Sam Snead the winning golfer in the history of the PGA Tour. Above: Snead won tournaments in four decades—the 1930s, '40s, '50s, and '60s— remarkable evidence of his ability and longevity. He became the first golfer to shoot his age or better when he shot rounds of 67 and 66 at the age of sixty-seven in the 1979 Quad Cities Open.*

Above: Curtis Strange spent the beginning of his professional career escaping from sand traps and learning to manage his estimable game and combustible emotions. Opposite page: Strange understands the reality of golf. He says, "The worst thing you can do in this game is begin to believe you are bullet proof, because we all go into slumps."

Curtis Strange

WILLIE ANDERSON OF SCOTLAND was three consecutive lines of small print in *Ye Auld Book of Golfe Records* until Curtis Strange won two consecutive U.S. Opens. Then Willie Anderson became a target. In 1990, Strange shot at Anderson and the mark of three successive open championships Anderson won in an era long ago, when golf clubs were hickory sticks and the cores of golf balls seemed to be made of marshmallow instead of solid rubber.

Strange and Willie Anderson did not end up sharing space on the same page of golf history books because Hale Irwin, an antique athlete of forty-five, won the 1990 Open title, his third, at Medinah Country Club near Chicago, Illinois. Strange was two shots behind entering the fourth round, but went out in thirty-eight and wound up sharing seventh place with Ian Woosnam and Steve Elkington.

Strange still deserves recognition, though, because in 1989, at Oak Hill Country Club in upstate New York, he did what golf geniuses, such as Jack Nicklaus, Arnold Palmer, Lee Trevino, Gary Player, and Tom Watson, were unable to do in their careers, and what merely five men in eighty-eight previous opens did: repeat as champion.

Jack Nicklaus won four open titles, but never two in a row. John McDermott (1911–12), Bobby Jones (1929–1930), Ralph Guldahl (1937–1938), and Ben Hogan (1950–1951) were the other golfers aside from Strange and Anderson to be in position to achieve the U.S. Open trifecta.

McDermott was eighth in the 1913 U.S. Open. Jones, worn down from competition and the pressure of being Unbeatable Bobby Jones, did not attempt to defend his titles. He chose instead to retire from golf. Guldahl was contending in the final round of the 1939 Open, but wound up seventh. Hogan was the leader halfway through the 1952 U.S. Open, but came in third, five shots behind the titlist, Julius Boros.

"I'm not sure what it means to do what I've done," Strange says. "I'm proud of it, naturally, but whether that makes me a great player, or number one in the country, I'm not real comfortable with that. The worst thing you can do in this game is begin to believe you're bulletproof, because we all go into slumps. The only golfer who hasn't, the only golfer who's owned it instead of renting it for a little while, is Jack Nicklaus."

Curtis Strange often can be as precise and emotionless as "Iron Byron," the mechanical swing duplicator. But he also has the kind of championship temperament and ability necessary to be more than just one of the anonymous and cautious golfers, the kind who are content collecting paychecks of any size.

Strange spent the early part of his professional career learning to manage his estimable game and combustible emotions. He had been an exceptional collegiate and amateur golfer, but all his promise did was make failure more difficult to accept.

Qualifying for the PGA Tour in 1976 surely was a gimmie for someone with his pedigree. But Strange was not among the Q-school graduates in his first attempt.

"You come on the tour as a twenty-one-year-old hotshot," Strange says, "and you think you can do no wrong. But after you've finished your amateur career, you go from the top of the totem pole to the bottom. And it's a big blow to your self-esteem to find out you can't compete for everything like you did just a day earlier."

Strange lost more tournaments than he won

© David Joyner/Bob Thomas Sports Photography

until the beginning of the 1980s, when his career took off like a perfectly struck tee ball. He led the PGA Tour in earnings three times in four years, beginning in 1985. In 1988, the year he won his first U.S. Open, Strange won four tournaments and was the first pro golfer to amass more than $1 million in one season.

He outshot Nick Faldo of England in a playoff to win the 1988 U.S. Open at the Country Club in Brookline, Massachusetts. The victory there was more valuable to him than the prize money, because it gave him prominence. Confidence, too.

Winning the open freed him from awful memories of the 1985 Masters, where he was three shots ahead in the final round until miscalculating the power necessary to reach the devilish thirteenth green. He mishit his second shot on the par-5 and lost his golf ball in the drink. He eventually lost the tournament to Bernhard Langer of Germany.

In 1989, Strange was the U.S. Open survivor by one shot. When pars were as good as birdies or better in the final round at Oak Hill, he made fifteen of them. His birdie at Number 16 gave him the cushion necessary to withstand a bogey at Number 18 and win an exacting open. Several able and affluent golfers, including the richest of them all, Tom Kite, lost their aim and their leads in the fourth round, enabling Strange to scale the pile of bodies of prospective open champions and ascend to the top of the leader board.

Curtis Strange is past thirty, the baleful age when many professional athletes begin losing their skills and desire. But Jack Nicklaus's victory in the 1986 Masters, at the age of forty-six, was proof of golfers' agelessness. Nicklaus's victory at Augusta did more to revive older athletes than six hours of whirlpool treatments. What all this means is Strange believes he did not leave his best golf at the Country Club or Oak Hill.

Lee Trevino

L EE TREVINO ALWAYS HAS BEEN PART gambler, part entertainer, and part golfer. In his youth, Trevino would rove Texas's scrubbier public golf courses with a makeshift club—a heavily taped Dr. Pepper bottle with a shaft through its long neck—searching for a pigeon and a match.

"I can beat you and your full bag of clubs with this ol' bottle" was his frequent challenge.

He always has been that confident. And he was usually that good, too. But the quarry has been known to occasionally outsmart the fearless pursuer.

Orville Moody, another professional golfer of note, enjoys recalling the time Trevino went pigeon hunting in the Far East more than thirty years ago. It seems Moody spent virtually all of his brief Army career at the driving range rather than at the shooting range. Indeed, when he was Sergeant Moody, about all he shot at was the pin; Moody was the unofficial golf professional at Camp Zama in Japan in 1959. His favorite war story involves him and Private Lee Trevino, then the captain of the traveling Marine golf team.

"He came from Okinawa into the pro shop one day," Moody says, "and he stood at the counter and said, 'I hear the sarge is around here.' I told him, 'You're looking at him, son.'"

Trevino was nineteen years old and about as thin as a one-iron, but even then he was all business. In no time, a match, and its passionate mood, was set.

"He was this little guy," Moody recalls. "He was very, very good. But I was, too. I told him, 'Son, it wouldn't be fair for me to take you and your partner on even up. So I'll play both of you, and you guys can hit your better ball.' I remember he fell backwards in shock."

Trevino could not believe the terms of the, well, business arrangement. What startled him more afterward was the outcome of the competition.

Moody says, "I beat him and his partner for seven consecutive days. He went up to my general afterwards and told him, 'Sir, I don't know why that guy isn't playing the tour.'"

Moody eventually did join the PGA Tour and even won the U.S. Open in 1969, the year after Trevino won the first of his two national titles by shooting four consecutive rounds in the sixties, a feat unmatched in golfing history.

In all, Trevino won six major championships and more than $3.5 million during his PGA Tour career. But his accomplishments did not alter the perception of him as someone who was three clubs short of a full bag, or left of center on the fairway of life.

Above: Varying terrains do not bother Lee Trevino, who can steer his golf ball through the narrowest and nastiest of openings. Opposite page: Trevino has been flashing his winning smile on the PGA and Senior tours for some twenty-five years.

Trevino, a headliner on the Senior Tour nowadays, still is different from the majority of PGA Tour members, but he is no oddball. He simply is a flask of Southern Comfort hidden in a dusty wine cellar, a pair of comfortable jeans on a rack of scratchy, plaid, double-knit trousers.

Trevino's informality on golf courses worldwide is not camouflage. He seems like someone you could slap on the back, charge to the nearest bar with, and chug some beers. He probably would lead the way.

Talkativeness distinguishes Trevino from his peers on the PGA and Senior tours. He usually entertains his audience with a comic monologue before beginning his workday, differentiating himself from the seemingly generic PGA pros, many of whom arrive on tour in a trance and can make conversation only with their bankers.

So many pros appear to be wound tighter than a golf ball; Trevino says all the gabbing, all the kibitzing, actually relaxes him. His casualness and composure are his signature qualities, have been since 1967, and probably will be until he retires sometime in the twenty-first century.

He beat Jack Nicklaus by three shots in a play-off for the 1972 U.S. Open and won a pair of PGA Championships ten years apart (1974 and 1984). In 1972 at Muirfield, he sank three chip shots and one bunker shot in the final round, and overtook Nicklaus on the seventy-first hole to win his second consecutive British Open title.

He is a supernatural shot maker. A club is a magic wand in his hands. Trevino strikes the ball and, presto, the result is usually the shot his imagination conjures. He can direct a golf ball either right or left, whatever direction is necessary to steer it toward the cup. Trevino can still work a golf ball as expertly as he works the crowd.

He was the low scorer on the PGA Tour five times—winning the Vardon Trophy every year from 1970 to 1972 and again in 1974 and 1980. In 1990, Trevino was old enough to join the Senior Tour, actually the Señor Tour. Super Mex, after all, did dominate his opponents in his first year of eligibility.

"How did I prepare for this tournament?" Trevino asked after overtaking Nicklaus in the championship round of the 1990 U.S. Senior Open. "Well, I'll tell ya: I won five tournaments and finished second three times."

Trevino was being amusing. He also was being honest. In six months he won seven tournaments and $1,190,518, a Senior Tour record, and almost $400,000 more than the old mark held by Bob Charles of New Zealand.

In actuality, he won the lottery without buying a ticket. The winning number was fifty, the age that qualified him as an authentic athletic antique, but also a senior golfer. His Senior Tour membership card was the equivalent of a bank card in 1990. In most cases, senior tournaments were another opportunity to present Trevino with an enormous paycheck.

"I love the competition, need the competition," he says.

On the Senior Tour, Lee Trevino, the comic magician, has become what Nicklaus was on the regular tour in his prime: the main attraction.

© Sam C. Pierson Jr.

Lee Trevino: *"There are two things not long for this world: dogs that chase cars and golfers who chip for pars."*

Caddies carry clubs and also the burden of helping their employers. Sometimes the emotional baggage can be heavy, but victory makes the strain and struggle worthwhile. Left: Tom Watson and his caddie act like teammates while celebrating victory at the 1983 British Open. Above: Herman Mitchell, Lee Trevino's trusty caddie, has been toting clubs and reading greens for more than thirty years. He enjoys his job, but there is nothing poetic about his longevity.

THE CADDIE

■

The best caddies are more than golfers' personal porters. The best caddies are advisers, psychologists…and bodyguards on occasion, too. In the last two rounds of the 1986 U.S. Open at Shinnecock Hills in New York, Herman Mitchell was part caddie, part sentry. His laser glares into the eyes of the loudmouths were effective enough to silence the rambunctious gallery and singe the fringe. Protecting Lee Trevino from distractions and hecklers on the golf course was one of his functions.

"I figure," Trevino said then, "if the gallery ever gets too rowdy and storms the restraining ropes, those people will have to get by Herman first. That will take them awhile—Herman weighs three hundred plus…at least three hundred plus. By then I'll be five hundred yards away."

Needling from Trevino does not hurt Mitchell, because the two of them have been business partners of sorts, and friends, since 1977. Mitchell knows joking playfully is part of Trevino's personality and his method of relaxing on the course.

"I'm a good caddie. Lee trusts me completely, and I trust him completely. Lee puts one hundred percent faith in me. We work together."

Professional golfers often entrust more than their clubs to their caddie. Professional golfers often entrust the direction of their careers to their caddie.

Mitchell says, "When I was Miller Barber's caddie, it was my job to lead him, and he knew I could."

Caddies essentially are paid to lug clubs, select clubs, pull clubs, help judge distances, and read greens. Caddies are occasionally support systems, too. Disconsolate professional golfers in slumps often want encouragement or inspiration, along with the correct weapon to attack the course, from their caddies.

"Face it, caddies sometimes are psychiatrists," Mitchell says. "Sometimes you have to listen to your guy's griping or crying."

Mitchell was not referring to Trevino, he says.

"I wish I could say I've brought something to his game. Lee's a champion. I consider myself lucky to be with him. He's been awfully good for me. There are an awful lot of good players, but not many champions."

Mitchell undervalues himself when he says, "We talk most of the time on the course. I help him. But I know Lee could win without me."

Trevino manages his game better than most pros. But Mitchell often provides him with either another opinion, or reassurance that his decision is correct—and confidence is as important as clean clubs to professional golfers.

"I'm going to be wrong sometimes," Mitchell confesses, "and he's going to be wrong sometimes, too. We can't help but be wrong. We're human."

Business relationships between pros and caddies, mergers of sorts, seldom last too long. Disinterest, incompetence, or incompatibility, on either side or both, usually are the reasons such associations end.

Mitchell has been carrying clubs and reading the grain of greens more than thirty years. There is nothing poetic about his longevity, though.

"It's a job, nothing extra," he says. "I began caddying when I was nine years old, but never thought about making a living at it. I couldn't find a job when I was discharged from the Navy, and one day an old friend of mine talked me into following him to a professional golf tournament. I carried the bag of one of the pros, stayed with him for a while, then moved on."

He has been a caddie and confidant for, among others, Gardner Dickinson (almost eight years), Miller Barber (almost three years), and now Trevino.

Trevino, a corporate raider of a sort, one day made Mitchell an offer, and Mitchell left Barber.

"Miller didn't like it," Mitchell says, "but it's not like we had a contract. When Lee asked me to be his caddie, it was like asking me whether I like bologna or steak. I like steak. In the past, I'd always had good players. I wanted to caddie for a superstar."

The best caddies working with the best golfers can earn plenty of money and even a portion of fame. Spectators recognize Mitchell because they know his boss, Trevino, who led the Senior Tour in victories (seven) and earnings (nearly $1.2 million) in 1990.

"I'm doing better than I've ever done in my life," he says. "I'm well known because of Lee," and well paid because of his business partnership with the headliner of the Senior Tour.

© David Cannon/Allsport

Tom Watson

H E ALREADY HAD WON FIVE MAJOR championships and more than $2 million, but Tom Watson was just another good golfer until he sank the shot of his life and won the 1982 U.S. Open with Jack Nicklaus chasing him.

Winning the U.S. Open is the equivalent of winning the World Series or the Super Bowl. Lives and judgments change because the world is watching. "Every golfer wants to win a major tournament," Watson says, "and the biggest of all is the open."

Watson won the Masters in 1977 and 1981 and the British Open in 1975, 1977, and 1980, but he was not in Nicklaus's class or on Nicklaus's level until he won his first open.

Nicklaus was in the scorers' tent accepting congratulations when Watson was in trouble on the seventeenth hole, a dangerous par-3 at Pebble Beach Golf Links in Pebble Beach, California. His ball was nearly invisible, embedded in deep emerald rough bisecting two bunkers to the left of the cup. Watson was sharing first with Nicklaus, but in his position, four was more likely than two or even three.

There's no way in the world he can get it up and down from there, Nicklaus was thinking.

Nicklaus was correct. Watson did not need two shots to complete the hole. One was enough. Watson sank the chip from seventeen feet, then did a victory lap around the green. The world did a double take, unable to believe the surprise ending to the tournament.

"It was an impossible shot," Bill Rogers was saying afterward. Rogers began the fourth round in first place with Watson. "You could let someone, anyone, hit a hundred balls from there, and they wouldn't hole one."

Watson turned a bogey into a birdie with one flick of his magical wedge.

"It was the greatest shot of my life, certainly the most meaningful. I hit it soft, and when it hit the green, I said, 'That's in the hole.'

"I practiced that shot for hours and hours. I told my caddy, 'I'm not going to try to get it close. I'm going to try to get it in.'"

Watson had lost the open at Pebble Beach before—in both practice rounds and in his mind.

"When I was younger, I'd drive down here from Stanford (University) and tee it up at seven A.M., when I'd have the course to myself. Honestly, I didn't fantasize about coming down the stretch head to head with Jack Nicklaus in the U.S. Open. I'd get to the last couple of holes and say, 'You've got to play these one under par to win the open.' Of course, I'd always play them two over. Then I'd say, 'You've got a long way to go, kid.'"

Under pressure and championship conditions he did not fail. He sank a birdie putt at Number 18 and won the tournament by two shots.

He won his fourth British Open in 1982 and his fifth in 1983. In 1984, Watson was chasing history, the ghost of Harry Vardon, a record sixth British Open title, his third in succession, when he reached the seventeenth hole, the Road Hole, at St. Andrews, in the fourth round of the tournament.

He lost the title and the chance to tie Vardon when he made bogey from the fairway and Sevé Ballesteros somehow made par from the fiendish Scottish whin. Watson has been slumping since then in major championships, coming out of it only long enough to challenge Scott Simpson in the 1987 U.S. Open at the Olympic Club and Ian Woosnam at the 1991 Masters.

Watson found his lost putting stroke in San Francisco, but his birdie attempt from forty feet away to tie Simpson came up an inch short on the seventy-second hole.

"I can't say I'm ashamed," he was saying afterward. "But I sure am disappointed."

Tom Watson may never win another open, but in 1982 he won his open. He got the trophy and posterity got one of the greatest shots in golf history.

Opposite page: Tom Watson was the leading money winner on the PGA Tour from 1977 through '80 and its Player of the Year a record six times. Right: His best season was 1980, when Watson won six PGA tournaments, the British Open, and earned $530,808, a money record at the time.

© David Cannon/Allsport

Kathy Whitworth

HER POKER FACE OFTEN READ A PAIR OF
twos when Kathy Whitworth usually had
thrown four aces down on the table to collect another pot. JoAnne Carner, like Whitworth a
member of the LPGA Hall of Fame, remembers
one of her rivals, "griping all the time. There she
was, shooting sixty-eight or sixty-seven and com-
plaining all the way. You'd swear she was shooting
seventy-nine. But I know now that was just Kathy
striving for perfection."

Whitworth apparently was wound tighter
than the core of a golf ball when she was competing full-time and winning regularly on the LPGA
Tour. She always was so business-like on a golf
course, because golf never was just a hobby to her.

"I'm not really trained to do anything other
than play golf," Whitworth says.

Winning golf tournaments was her sole
ambition, and in all Whitworth has won eighty-
eight of them, more than any professional golfer
in history.

The odds of her ending up as the most successful professional golfer in history were not as
long as any U.S. Open course, but history certainly
did not favor Whitworth, either. Her swing was
downright unusual, first of all—too upright, too
loose, too much weight on her left side. And while
Whitworth could putt, she was nothing more
than an anonymous amateur from Monahans,
Texas, before joining the LPGA in 1958.

Carner remembers unknowingly competing
in the same amateur tournament with Whitworth
in 1958 and then not understanding the com-
motion when an official told her excitedly:
"Whitworth's turning pro." "Who?" Carner says
was her honest reply.

All the fussing was puzzling to Carner, since
she was the top female amateur golfer in America
at the time. Carner won the U.S. Junior Championship in 1956, and was the defending U.S. Amateur
titlist. All Whitworth had done in her career was
finish first in the 1957 and 1958 New Mexico State
Amateur Championships.

Golfers good enough to advance to the professional level usually drive up to their first tournament inside a fancy car with an assortment of

hood ornaments in the trunk—actually an array of trophies won at amateur tournaments across the country. Whitworth did not enter the pros with the same sort of hardware collection. "Most of the really good players on the LPGA Tour compiled terrific amateur records," says Carner, who ought to know, since she won five U.S. Amateur titles, a record, before finally joining the LPGA Tour in 1970, at the age of thirty.

"Turning pro for them was the natural progression. They knew they could be the best again, because they already had been as teenagers. Kathy did not have that strong amateur background, so what she's accomplished on the tour is amazing."

Whitworth, fifty-two, did not leave any clues of her future achievements her first season. Her performance was proof that golf is not as easy as it looks, even for the pros.

Her scoring average was excessive (80.3) and her winnings in twenty-six events were an unimpressive $1,217, or roughly what Beth Daniel probably spent tipping valet parkers from her earnings of nearly $864,000 in 1990.

Whitworth finally won her first tournament in 1962, at the Kelly Girl Open. The victory spigot opened; she won eight tournaments in 1963, one in 1964, eight in 1965, nine in 1966, eight in 1967, ten in 1968, and eight more in 1969. The victories were worth confidence, prestige, and plenty of money. In every season except one from 1965 through 1973, Whitworth led the LPGA in earnings. In 1981, she became the first female golfer to reach $1 million in career prize money.

In April 1982, at the CPC International, she easily won her eighty-second tournament, drawing even with Mickey Wright. Reaching her goal was easier than explaining the accomplishment. "You think, 'Why me? How come I was the one to win so many tournaments?'" she says.

The answer is confidence. In her prime, Whitworth always was sure she could win golf tournaments. Golfers without confidence have as much chance of succeeding as they do of sinking a putt from fifty-five feet with a sand wedge.

"Kathy always put a lot of pressure on herself to be the best," Carner says. "Her swing was awkward, but it produced results."

Wright and Whitworth did not share the same page of the LPGA record book too long—Whitworth won her eighty-third tournament at

© Howard O. Allen

the Lady Michelob in May 1982. She won five more tournaments before her game began unraveling in 1987.

"She did fabulously to last so long," Carner says. "No one's going to break her record. Why? There's too much competition these days, and, because there's so much more money nowadays, the players' attitudes are different.

"Players consider three victories a great year, and anything over three an exceptional year."

Kathy Whitworth hides her success behind a bronzed, expressionless poker face, but Whitworth reveals a little bit of herself and her record with her apt choice of hometowns. Whitworth nowadays lives in Trophy Club, Texas.

Opposite page: Kathy Whitworth may have an imperfect swing, but she has the perfect championship temperament. She has won the most tournaments of any professional golfer—woman or man—eighty-eight. Above: Whitworth is the most decorated golfer in LPGA history. She has been the leading money winner eight times, Player of the Year seven times, and Vare Trophy winner, emblematic of the lowest scoring average, seven times.

© Sam C. Pierson Jr.

MINORITIES IN GOLF

■

The color of golf began changing subtly in 1990. Until then, golf had been primarily as white as the standard ball.

There still are many more black caddies than black professional golfers or black members at country clubs. Significant differences in the shading of the game were noticeable at the end of 1990, anyway, particularly when black executives, Ron Townsend and Louis Willie, became members at exclusive, and theretofore exclusionary, clubs: Townsend at Augusta National, the sacrosanct house of golf in Augusta, Georgia, and Willie at Shoal Creek in Birmingham, Alabama.

Restrictive policies at private clubs is an old issue, but was not a volatile national issue until June 1990. Invitations to Townsend and Willie were the surprising reaction to, and result of, an intolerable declaration of bigotry made then by Hall Thompson, founder of Shoal Creek Country Club.

"The country club is our home," Thompson said prior to the 1990 PGA Championship at Shoal Creek, "and we pick and choose who we want. That sort of thing just doesn't happen in Birmingham....We have Jews, women, Lebanese, and Italians—but not blacks."

The statement was ugly enough to repulse many major corporate sponsors—who withdrew advertisements from the golf tournament—and incense black organizations.

The response from many leading PGA players was either synthetic disapproval, smug concern, or outright timidity. Courses ought not discriminate was the tough consensus reply from most pros, but their collective follow-through was terribly weak—implicit defense of "Mr. Thompson and his opinion."

"We are golfers, not politicians" was the nearly unanimous proclamation from PGA pros. The implication was that professional golfers form some sort of subculture of human beings and are freed from having social consciences.

Payne Stewart essentially was the pros' spokesman, saying, "The players probably have made more jokes about it than anything else."

Among the exceptions were Lee Trevino and 1987 U.S. Open champion, Scott Simpson. Trevino, who won the PGA Championship at Shoal Creek in 1984, thought about dropping out of the event, but in the end wound up competing.

Simpson said, "This isn't right. This doesn't do anybody any good. We need more minority participation in golf, not less."

There were no protest demonstrations during the PGA Championship because Shoal Creek agreed to accept its first black member, thus replacing the pin in a live grenade. Louis Willie, president of Booker T. Washington Insurance Company, originally was uncomfortable with his status as pioneer. He thought the offer initially was more symbolic than significant. Willie rethought his position later, though.

"There's a lot of history involved," he says. "My acceptance at Shoal Creek was another indication of equal access. In the United States, in the 1990s, it is nonsense to be denied entry into a country club because of the color of skin."

Willie was chosen because of his prominence in Birmingham, not because of his proficiency at the game. He grew up enjoying golf, but his exposure to the game was on a scrubby course set aside for blacks, "a course," he says, "on which it often was difficult to differentiate the fairways and greens from the rough."

Willie became an honorary member at Shoal Creek in August 1990, but did not have enough time to play the course before the end of the season, because he spent so much time telling writers from across the country what amounts to his acceptance speech.

"I can't say I enjoyed all the publicity," he says. "I thought there were three candidates more worthy, and I told that to the membership committee at Shoal Creek. But what happened had to be done for the sake of the community."

Townsend, president of Gannett Television, and Willie were heroes of sorts, and also symbols of the sports world's overdue contiguous orbit with the real world.

The response to Shoal Creek was partly encouraging and partly discouraging: The USGA, PGA, and PGA of America drafted guidelines requiring clubs hosting their events to implement open membership policies.

But rather than comply with the outline, seven clubs, among them Cypress Point, Butler National, and Aronimink, withdrew as tournament sites. The PGA Tour, because of the withdrawals, lost two Senior PGA, two PGA Tour, and two Ben Hogan Tour events.

Golf has long been known as a man's game, indeed a white man's game. Charles Sifford was the first black man to compete regularly on the PGA Tour, but not until 1962, fifteen years after the integration of major-league baseball.

Sifford, a member of the Senior PGA Tour nowadays, won two tournaments during his PGA career—the 1967 Hartford Open and the 1969 Los Angeles Open—but never did receive an invitation to the Masters. It was not until 1975 that Lee Elder became the first black to tee up in the Masters.

Sifford has belonged to a private club— Deerwood near Houston, Texas—since 1988.

"I joined," he says, "because from the day I first walked in, the people there treated me like a human being. They showed me they're happy to have me out there."

His experience has been pleasant, but Sifford is skeptical about the further colorization of golf at private clubs.

"No man, black or white, wants to go where he's made to feel he's intruding," he says.

"Socially, it's just too difficult a situation, even for the blacks who are wealthy enough to join. They don't have to have rules to let you know you are intruding in their little party.

"A club might be pressured into letting you join, but after they take your twenty thousand dollars, how comfortable are you going to feel around people who constantly give you the cold shoulder, just because you have dark skin?"

How much more the color of golf changes in the future is difficult to predict, because so many club members across America, it seems, need to alter their attitudes about minorities, not adjust the wording on an application form.

© David Cannon/Allsport

Opposite page: *Charles Sifford was the first black man to compete regularly on the PGA Tour, fifteen long years after the integration of major league baseball. Above: Jim Thorpe, one of the most successful black golfers in history, grew up off the second fairway of the Roxboro (North Carolina) Golf Club. Thorpe says he and his father, Elvert, the greens superintendent at the course, used to go out after dark and hit shots by the back porch light.*

The Tournaments

Left: Sam Snead won more golf tournaments than Jack Nicklaus, Ben Hogan, Arnold Palmer, Byron Nelson, Walter Hagen, and Gene Sarazen. In fact, Snead won more tournaments than any golfer in PGA history. Opposite page: Golf can be an amusing diversion or a lonesome, stressful job. It also can be a rewarding occupation if one plays the game as well as Greg Norman (right).

© Bob Daemmrich/Allsport

TOP TEN VICTORIES

PGA
(CAREER THROUGH 1990)

Place	Name	No.
1.	Sam Snead	81
2.	Jack Nicklaus	70
3.	Ben Hogan	63
4.	Arnold Palmer	60
5.	Byron Nelson	52
6.	Billy Casper	51
7.	Walter Hagen	40
8.	Cary Middlecoff	40
9.	Gene Sarazen	38
10.	Lloyd Mangrum	36

© Sam C. Pierson Jr.

The PGA

GOLFERS GOOD ENOUGH TO JOIN THE Professional Golfers Association Tour generally are athletes keeping the long hours and living the tedious life-style of traveling salesmen. Sleeping in too many motels, eating too many meals in restaurants, and being hundreds of miles from girlfriends, wives, or families often can upset professional golfers more than missing par putts. But the PGA Tour can be as alluring as it is tiring.

"It reminds me of Circe, the ancient, mythological siren," Gary McCord of CBS says. "It's always enticing you with its life-style… not to mention the four dozen free golf balls and gloves per week the players receive from manufacturers."

Nowadays McCord talks about the game much more than he plays it. He is the most colorful of professional golf's TV color analysts. McCord always analyzes in primary colors, distinguishing him from most of his colleagues, who examine the sport in gray tones. "It's wonderful to have the golf course as your office," says McCord, who is a better pro golfer than he implies during broadcasts. "The guys unlucky enough to lose their PGA privileges usually do whatever it takes to return to the tour and their dream."

The incredible earning potential of pro golfers nowadays seduces such people. In 1934, the year PGA bookkeepers began recording such figures, total prize money in thirty-eight tournaments was $158,000. These days, first place is worth more than that in plenty of tournaments.

When Byron Nelson won eleven tournaments in succession in 1945, his take was $30,250 —good money, but hardly a jackpot. The same

feat today would generate a reward of $2 million or more.

The golfing gods choose the keepers of the secret discriminately. The PGA Tour is not made up of 125 Curtis Stranges, Greg Normans, Fred Couples, Mark Calcavecchias, or Payne Stewarts. The typical pro chases golf balls and boyhood dreams on beautiful courses worldwide, without becoming a tycoon.

There was a time, though, when professional golf was more of a game than a business. Pro golf once was about accumulating trophies, acclaim, and good wages, instead of just bales of cash. In the frolicking Age of Golf, a time that was different, not necessarily better, players such as Byron Nelson, Walter Hagen, Gene Sarazen, Sam Snead, and Ben Hogan did not always impersonate businessmen.

These days, who can tell the difference between many pro golfers and corporate executives, even after careful examinations of their financial statements? The craving and capability to fill up bank vaults instead of trophy cases sometimes influences PGA golfers these days, meddling somewhat with the intent and image of the tour, though not enough to interfere with growing sponsorship of tournaments.

Winners' purses have become so large that one victory enables a champion to relax for several weeks. So the best golfer is not always the leading money winner anymore.

"I think some of the guys are just trying to make money, and I don't think our tour is here to provide a living for one hundred guys," says Lanny Wadkins, who is even more aggressive than rich, and he has won more than $5 million in his career.

"It's become too easy to stay out here. A lot of guys just want to win money, and it ought to be about winning tournaments, and not having a victory dropped in your lap with everyone else backing off."

Financial security is depriving some PGA golfers of their competitive edge and creating the impression that European golfers are better.

"Actually," Jack Nicklaus says, "we have more good golfers in the U.S., but they're not the predominant players. They make a lot of money without winning many tournaments, so our guys are not learning how to win consistently."

PGA Championship

Year	Name	Score	Year	Name	Score	Year	Name	Score
1916	James M. Barnes	1 up	1941	Vic Ghezzi	1 up	1966	Al Geiberger	280
1917	No tournament; World War I		1942	Sam Snead	2 and 1	1967	*Don January (69)	281
1918	No tournament; World War I		1943	No tournament; World War II		1968	Julius Boros	281
1919	James M. Barnes	6 and 5	1944	Bob Hamilton	1 up	1969	Ray Floyd	276
1920	Jock Hutchison	1 up	1945	Byron Nelson	4 and 3	1970	Dave Stockton	279
1921	Walter Hagen	3 and 2	1946	Ben Hogan	6 and 4	1971	Jack Nicklaus	281
1922	Gene Sarazen	4 and 3	1947	Jim Ferrier	2 and 1	1972	Gary Player	281
1923	Gene Sarazen	1 up	1948	Ben Hogan	7 and 6	1973	Jack Nicklaus	277
1924	Walter Hagen	2 up	1949	Sam Snead	3 and 2	1974	Lee Trevino	276
1925	Walter Hagen	6 and 5	1950	Chandler Harper	4 and 3	1975	Jack Nicklaus	276
1926	Walter Hagen	5 and 3	1951	Sam Snead	3 and 2	1976	Dave Stockton	281
1927	Walter Hagen	1 up	1952	Jim Turnesa	1 up	1977	**Lanny Wadkins	282
1928	Leo Diegel	6 and 5	1953	Walter Burkemo	2 and 1	1978	**John Mahaffey	276
1929	Leo Diegel	6 and 4	1954	Chick Harbert	4 and 3	1979	**David Graham	272
1930	Tommy Armour	1 up	1955	Doug Ford	4 and 3	1980	Jack Nicklaus	274
1931	Tom Creavy	2 and 1	1956	Jack Burke	3 and 2	1981	Larry Nelson	273
1932	Olin Dutra	4 and 3	1957	Lionel Hebert	2 and 1	1982	Ray Floyd	272
1933	Gene Sarazen	5 and 4	1958	Dow Finsterwald	276	1983	Hal Sutton	274
1934	Paul Runyan	1 up	1959	Bob Rosburg	277	1984	Lee Trevino	273
1935	Johnny Revolta	5 and 4	1960	Jay Hebert	281	1985	Hubert Green	278
1936	Denny Shute	3 and 2	1961	*Jerry Barber (67)	277	1986	Bob Tway	276
1937	Denny Shute	1 up	1962	Gary Player	278	1987	**Larry Nelson	287
1938	Paul Runyan	8 and 7	1963	Jack Nicklaus	279	1988	Jeff Sluman	272
1939	Henry Picard	1 up	1964	Bobby Nichols	271	1989	Payne Stewart	276
1940	Byron Nelson	1 up	1965	Dave Marr	280	1990	Wayne Grady	282

*Winner in play-off, score in parentheses.

**Winner in sudden-death play-off.

TOP TEN MONEY WINNERS

PGA
(CAREER THROUGH 1990)

Place	Name	Earnings
1.	Tom Kite	$6,258,893
2.	Tom Watson	$5,374,232
3.	Curtis Strange	$5,272,892
4.	Jack Nicklaus	$5,170,465
5.	Lanny Wadkins	$4,614,381
6.	Payne Stewart	$4,582,988
7.	Ben Crenshaw	$4,466,267
8.	Greg Norman	$4,251,270
9.	Hale Irwin	$4,066,080
10.	Ray Floyd	$3,880,665

Left: *Sand on his workclothes doesn't bother Tom Kite—he can afford to send them to the dry cleaners, since he has won more money than any golfer in PGA history.*

The LPGA

W HEN THE LPGA WAS YOUNGER AND
purses were meager, Marlene Hagge,
one of the charter members, pur-
chased and shared a purple gingham cocktail
dress with five other golfers, including Jane Blalock and Judy Rankin. The six women alternated
wearing the dress to parties.

Hagge smiles when remembering the story,
because, after all, it is an entertaining anecdote
and proof of how much progress the LPGA has
made since its founding in 1950.

LPGA members share millions and millions
of dollars in prize money nowadays. The best
women golfers can afford closets full of party
dresses and baubles the size and circumference of
golf balls. Beth Daniel won seven tournaments
and nearly $870,000 in prize money in 1990. Total
purses did not top $1 million until 1973.

The association has its troubles—fluctuating
leadership, competition from the old-timers on
the Senior Tour, and a lack of airtime on national
television. Commissioner Charles Mechem hopes
to use his expertise and connections to help the
LPGA gain more exposure on TV, but women
consistently landing golf balls on the middle of
fairways and the middle of greens apparently bore
TV producers. Women golfers need to be super-
models, too, in order to attract the attention of
viewers, the eyes of cameras, and more coverage.

Men launching golf balls over traps and
ponds, around trees, and nearly into coincidental
orbits with Jupiter appeal to people who produce
golf tournaments. It helps that long drives in the
country suggest automobiles, whose manufacturers are among the major sponsors of golf
tournaments.

"Our big problem is everybody expects all
of us to be able to hit the ball as far as men," says
JoAnne Carner, an LPGA member since 1970, a
Hall of Fame inductee in 1982, and once one of
the longest hitters on the tour. "Lee Trevino was
the first broadcaster to understand holes as short
as 380 yards weren't easy for all women. Trevino
didn't act surprised and wasn't condescending
when he saw women approaching a 380-yard
hole with four-irons."

THE TOURNAMENTS ◄ 69

TOP TEN VICTORIES

LPGA
(CAREER THROUGH 1990)

Place	Name	No.
1.	Kathy Whitworth	88
2.	Mickey Wright	82
3.	Patty Berg	57
4.	Betsy Rawls	55
5.	Louise Suggs	50
6.	Nancy Lopez	43
7.	JoAnne Carner	42
8.	Carol Mann	38
9.	Babe Zaharias	31
10.	Jane Blalock	29

Opposite page: Marlene Hagge was one of the first LPGA standouts. She wanted to play for a living and did so, beginning at the age of sixteen. She remains the youngest woman to join the LPGA and the youngest, at age eighteen, to win an LPGA tournament. Right: Beth Daniel is one of the stars of the tour these days.

© Maria Veghte/Visuals Unlimited

TOP TEN MONEY WINNERS

LPGA
(CAREER THROUGH 1990)

Place	Name	Earnings
1.	Pat Bradley	$3,346,047
2.	Nancy Lopez	$3,026,470
3.	Betsy King	$3,013,537
4.	Beth Daniel	$2,893,482
5.	Patty Sheehan	$2,830,464
6.	Amy Alcott	$2,491,855
7.	JoAnne Carner	$2,386,887
8.	Ayako Okamoto	$2,042,466
9.	Jan Stephenson	$1,832,085
10.	Kathy Whitworth	$1,719,804

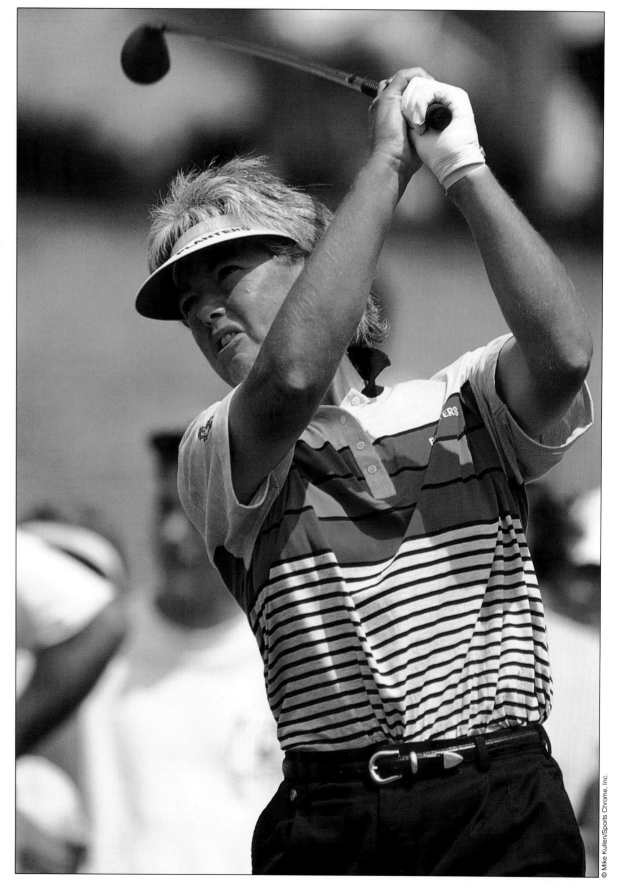

Earning a good living was difficult in the early years of the LPGA Tour, but huge increases in purses and the popularity of women's golf, along with their own abilities, have enabled Pat Bradley (right) and Beth Daniel (opposite page) to become tycoons.

© Mike Kullen/Sports Chrome, Inc.

LPGA Championship

Year	Name	Score	Year	Name	Score
1955	**Beverly Hanson (4 and 3)	220	1975	Kathy Whitworth	288
1956	†Marlene Hagge	291	1976	Betty Burfeindt	287
1957	Louise Suggs	285	1977	Chako Higuchi	279
1958	Mickey Wright	288	1978	Nancy Lopez	275
1959	Betsy Rawls	288	1979	Donna Caponi	279
1960	Mickey Wright	292	1980	Sally Little	285
1961	Mickey Wright	287	1981	Donna Caponi	279
1962	Judy Kimball	282	1982	Jan Stephenson	279
1963	Mickey Wright	294	1983	Patty Sheehan	279
1964	Mary Mills	278	1984	Patty Sheehan	272
1965	Sandra Haynie	279	1985	Nancy Lopez	273
1966	Gloria Ehret	282	1986	Pat Bradley	277
1967	Kathy Whitworth	284	1987	Jane Geddes	275
1968	*Sandra Post (68)	294	1988	Sherri Turner	281
1969	Betsy Rawls	293	1989	Nancy Lopez	274
1970	†Shirley Englehorn	285	1990	Beth Daniel	207
1971	Kathy Whitworth	288			
1972	Kathy Ahern	293			
1973	Mary Mills	288			
1974	Sandra Haynie	288			

*Winner in play-off, score in parentheses.
**Winner of match-play final.
†Hagge and Englehorn won play-offs in sudden death.

Besides more power hitters, the LPGA needs an identity, critics say. "Identity" is a code word meaning the LPGA needs someone who can win tournaments, belt the ball pin high, and act as a poster pinup, too. In 1990, golf producer/director Frank Chirkinian did not resort to cryptography. He essentially told a magazine interviewer what the LPGA needs is another champion/sex symbol, another Jan Stephenson.

"The last few years [the LPGA] has had some dynamite-looking girls out there playing golf. And that's what the sport really needs…some striking female to take over and become the next superstar. It would have been Nancy Lopez, but Nancy turned to motherhood and so has her body."

Carner would not object to seeing a beauty pageant winner who can also sink putts from twenty-five feet succeed on the tour, because such a person would continue to improve the image of women athletes.

"What would be so wrong with that?" she asks. "People need to realize women can be feminine and athletic at the same time. The LPGA is so much better than when I began my career. The scores are so much lower, and we did not have the depth back then, either. When I was starting, there were maybe five or six players capable of winning. Nowadays, there are nineteen or twenty different winners."

Galleries ought to appreciate the accuracy and talent of women golfers. Golf is not a home-run contest. "Drive for show and putt for dough" is the adage almost as old as the game. But that description of golf is hardly adequate. The best women golfers prove derringers are just as potent as cannons in the proper hands.

*J*an Stephenson is the pinup girl of golf and an excellent player. Some of her colleagues on the Ladies Professional Golfers Association Tour thought her fashion layouts in golf magazines during the early 1980s were demeaning. There also were people who thought the same pictures gave the LPGA necessary energy and publicity.

© WPGA/Allsport

© Budd Symes/Allsport

Opposite page: Jan Stephenson's picturesque swing and attractive profile made her wealthy and well known. She became the LPGA Tour's ninth millionaire in 1985 with a victory at the GNA Classic. She is the first woman professional to design golf courses. Left: Jane Blalock won twenty-nine tournaments from 1969 to 1985, and only the rigid qualifications stand between her and entry into the LPGA Hall of Fame. Blalock was the seventh LPGA millionaire and the first to earn $100,000 or more in four consecutive seasons.

*J*ane Blalock won the largest check of her career from her employer—the LPGA.

In 1972, Blalock's peers accused her of cheating (she allegedly marked her ball closer to the cup). Blalock was suspended and fined, but an appeals court found in her favor, and the LPGA had to both reinstate her and reimburse her $100,000.

Arnold Palmer (above) and Billy Casper (opposite page) were among the Big Four players of the regular PGA Tour in the 1950s and '60s. Palmer and Casper continue to compete and contend in golf tournaments nowadays because of the establishment of the PGA Senior Tour.

The Senior Tour

THE PGA SENIOR TOUR ORIGINALLY WAS a sentimental enterprise, but suddenly is a sports phenomenon that generates the kind of cash real-estate magnate Donald Trump owes monthly in interest payments.

Official prize money was $250,000 from two events in 1980. But in ten years, interest in older golfers has grown enormously, and so, too, has the size of Senior Tour purses. In 1990, nearly $18 million was given away to golfing relics in forty-three tournaments.

"This is a tour with a message," Gary Player says. "It's about longevity."

Until recently, growing old never was so rewarding.

"I have never seen anything blow up like this," says former Masters champion Doug Ford, one of the men behind the promotion and development of the Senior Tour. "Whatever we've done has worked."

The tour has been so successful because the golfers, all fifty or older, provide the public with more than nostalgia, or an encore from their heroes. Galleries genuinely have fun watching Jack Nicklaus and Lee Trevino, the headliners of the Senior Tour nowadays, stage one more dogfight. In the 1990 U.S. Senior Open, a tournament Trevino won by two shots against Nicklaus, it was exhilarating reliving Merion 1971, when Trevino won his second U.S. Open Championship by defeating Nicklaus (68–71) in a play-off. Or Muirfield 1972, when Trevino beat Nicklaus again, and the grand prize was his second consecutive British Open title.

"Jack and Lee intimidate everybody a little bit, I think," Orville Moody says, and he is one of the most successful golfers on the tour.

But Nicklaus, since he has been on the regular tour since the 1980s, is only a ceremonial senior golfer.

"I'm in a quandary," Nicklaus says. "Play on the regular tour, play the Seniors, or not play at all. The Senior Tour is wonderful. My problem is that I feel I'm still competitive on the regular tour. I'm supposed to drop this and go to the Seniors just because I'm fifty?"

Nicklaus is the main attraction to any tournament he enters, but recognizable and popular names from leader boards of the 1960s fill up the leader boards of Senior tournaments today. Arnold Palmer, Gary Player, Billy Casper, Chi Chi Rodriguez, Jim Dent, Miller Barber, and George Archer are just a few.

"If you can't enjoy this, what's the point?" says Archer, one of the finest putters in golf history. "There's no pressure on me to make a living."

The tour, though, is more than a friendly retirement community for senior golfers. The Senior Tour is a place for serious golfers looking for second chances, second careers. Walt Zembriski, soldier-laborer-golfer, epitomizes the potential of the Senior Tour. He had an improbable dream when he was young, and since then he has had both the perseverance and the good fortune to achieve his goal. Zembriski has been chasing a dream and a golf ball since he was a teenager growing up in Mahwah, New Jersey. In his lifetime, Zembriski, fifty-five, has been an ironworker, a construction worker, a caddie, a soldier, and a clerk in a tack factory.

He always has been a good golfer, too. But until his fiftieth birthday, Zembriski, who won the New Jersey State Amateur Championship in 1966, never was good enough to earn a living at his favorite game, a compulsion he says his former wife did not understand.

In his first five years on the Senior Tour, Zembriski, who spent two winless and penniless years on the regular PGA Tour in the early 1960s, won three tournaments and more than $1.3 million.

"I play hard every day, and I've got no nerves," he says. "Once you've walked a six-inchwide beam fifty stories off the ground, a three-foot putt doesn't scare you."

© Bob Thomas Sports Photography

TOP TEN MONEY WINNERS

PGA SENIOR (CAREER THROUGH 1990)

Place	Name	Earnings
1.	Bob Charles	$2,494,732
2.	Miller Barber	$2,488,787
3.	Chi Chi Rodriguez	$2,235,159
4.	Bruce Crampton	$2,147,530
5.	Orville Moody	$2,136,180
6.	Gary Player	$2,111,928
7.	Don January	$1,813,545
8.	Dale Douglass	$1,768,120
9.	Harold Henning	$1,758,416
10.	Gene Littler	$1,540,366

© David Cannon/Allsport

Left: Golf swings, like the shape of golf courses, vary widely. Miller Barber (left) has one of the oddest back swings in history. Opposite page: Spectators willingly spend $20 or more to watch professionals launch golf balls into orbit—or sometimes at them.

WEIRD SWINGS

■

Miller Barber swings his golf club like a door with a loose hinge, but he has won almost $4 million since joining the Professional Golfers Association Tour in 1959.

Chi Chi Rodriguez slashes violently at the ball, as though he were hacking at sugarcane with a machete, the way his father made a tough living years ago in the Caribbean. The flaws in his swing did not prevent him from becoming a golfing millionaire.

Golfers do not have to swing like Ben Hogan to be successful. Rodriguez and Barber have two of the oddest swings in golfing history, but are among the most prosperous golfers of all time because the heads of their clubs usually are square at impact, rendering their initial mechanical mistakes meaningless.

Miller Barber: *"I don't say my golf game is bad; but if I grew tomatoes,
they'd come up sliced."*

Hale Irwin on the Masters: *"You start to choke when you drive through the front gate (of Augusta National). On the first hole, you just want to make contact with the ball."*

© David Joyner/Bob Thomas Sports Photography

Above: Memorable performances distinguish major championships from the regular tournaments of the PGA and LPGA tours. Hale Irwin, for instance, supposedly was too old to win the 1990 U.S. Open, but he won the title at the age of forty-five. Opposite page: Sevé Ballesteros knows the thrill of winning a major. He has won five of them (two Masters, three British Opens) in his career.

The Majors

P RACTICE ALWAYS IS BENEFICIAL, BUT is often boring. So to relieve some of the monotony, American Mike Donald remembers ending each workday with a game when he was younger.

"When I was growing up," Donald says, "I remember putting on the practice green with some other guys. The first long putt was to win the Masters, the second one was to win the U.S. Open, the third one was to win the British Open, and the fourth one was to win the PGA Championship. I recall even then trying to collect all four majors."

Practically all the golfers who earn their living on the PGA and LPGA tours want to excel in major tournaments (the U.S. Open, LPGA Championship, Dinah Shore, Du Maurier Classic for

women) because the world is watching them and judging them.

"The open was the most exciting thing that's ever happened to me," Donald says. "It's hard to put behind me…and in a way I don't want to put it behind me. I've got a tape of it. I know when I'm seventy years old, I'm still going to be inviting friends over to see the tape of me playing in the open."

The 1990 U.S. Open experience meant so much to Donald…and he wound up finishing second. Hale Irwin beat him with a birdie from eight feet at the ninety-first hole of the tournament. At the age of forty-five years, fifteen days, Irwin became the fourth male golfer to win more than two opens, and also the oldest open champion in golf history.

History, immortality, and memories, both sad and spectacular, are what differentiate the major tournaments from the golf bags full of exaggerated Corporate Classics on the PGA and LPGA tours.

"I'd like to win ten, twelve, fifteen majors," says Australian Greg Norman, who has been in contention to win several since 1984, but has won just the 1986 British Open.

In his childhood, Norman was always winning the Masters or British Open, tournaments he saw on TV.

"I still practice a lot that way," he says. "Standing on the practice tee, I'll say, 'I need to land this four-iron on the green and two-putt to win the British Open.'"

Spectators, experts, and archivists always remember the champions of majors—and sometimes those same people ought not forget the runners-up, because how someone loses in the majors sometimes can be more eventful and compelling than how someone succeeds in the majors. Patty Sheehan was nine strokes ahead of the 1990 U.S. Women's Open field at the end of two rounds, but she was ill and did not have the stamina to endure thirty-six holes on the final day of the tournament. Sheehan lost all of her lead, the tournament, and then her composure. She wept afterward, not because of all the money scores of 75 and 76 cost her, but because winning the open was her mission.

"I know one day I'm going to win a U.S. Open," said Sheehan, who came close to accom-

© David Cannon/Allsport

plishing her goal in 1983 and 1988. "But it's difficult knowing all I had to do was play solid, and I didn't."

Robert DeVicenzo lost the 1968 Masters to Bob Goalby because of a bookkeeping error. He made three on the seventeenth hole. His playing partner, Tommy Aaron, accidentally marked four on DeVicenzo's scorecard.

DeVicenzo approved the incorrect card, so he shot 35 instead of 34, and 66 instead of 65 for the final round. Instead of sharing first place with Goalby, he lost by one miscalculated shot.

"What a stupid I am," his unforgettable

response to the mistake, may end up being DeVicenzo's epitaph.

Some professional golfers today consider the major tournaments to be nothing more than another business trip, one more stop on their lucrative walking tour of America and the earth. But since golf is as much a tradition as it is a game, finishing anywhere other than first in major championships can downright haunt the great golfers.

Sam Snead won eighty-one golf tournaments on the PGA Tour—more than anybody —but none of them was the U.S. Open, and a one-club's length relief has never been enough

distance to separate him from his own failure. Nancy Lopez was in the LPGA Hall of Fame by the age of thirty without once winning the U.S. Women's Open, her one professional regret. The PGA Championship ought to change its name to the One Major Tournament Arnold Palmer Did Not Win. Tom Watson, incidentally, lacks the same prize in his trophy case. Tom Kite has won the most money of anybody in golf history, but never has cashed the winner's check in a major championship.

"Sometimes," Byron Nelson says, "major tournaments simply escape from outstanding players, and absolutely no one knows why."

The majors really are just tournaments with catchy and memorable nicknames and universal appeal. The attention of the world was drawn to them because of Jack Nicklaus's single-minded determination to win more of them than any pro. Nicklaus long ago displaced the old male leader, Walter Hagen. He did not stop accumulating majors until he had reached eighteen, three more than Patty Berg, the LPGA leader.

What really makes majors interesting is that sometimes the favorites lose to someone anonymous, someone with whom the cruel golfing gods taunt the Nicklauses, Palmers, Hogans, Lopezes, or Carners for one week. Jack Fleck went birdie-par-par-birdie from fifteen through eighteen in the final round of the 1955 Open at the Olympic Club in San Francisco to tie none other than Ben Hogan, and then beat him in a play-off. Orville Moody sounds like the name of the cantankerous sheriff in one of Burt Reynolds's *Smokey and the Bandit* films, but ol' Sarge actually was the 1969 Open champion. JoAnne Carner in 1987 was going to be the oldest woman to win the U.S. Women's Open, until she lost her putting stroke on the seventy-second hole, and eventually lost a play-off to Laura Davies, then unknown outside of England.

"That's the only tournament, to this day, I ever regret losing," Carner says. "I've lost a bunch of them in my career, but that's the only one that bothers me. I lost it mentally on the eighteenth green. I waited too long to strike the [par] putt. I had no idea of the speed or direction of the putt. It was just one of those mental lapses. In hindsight, I should have remembered no putt in a major championship is slow." Or easy.

Right: *Laura Davies of England, champion of the 1987 U.S. Women's Open, was one more previously unknown golfer who had an unbelievable week in a major tournament.* **Opposite page:** *Gary Player, a golfer with an appropriate name.*

Eight Golfers Born to Play the Game

1. Mark Lye
2. Chip Beck
3. Hubert Green
4. Ken Green
5. Gary Player
6. Tammie Green
7. Willie Wood
8. Craig Wood

Top Fifteen Golf Names

1. Forrest Fezler
2. Dow Finsterwald
3. Lance Ten Broeck
4. Duffy Waldorf
5. Webb Heintzelman
6. Beau Baugh
7. Gibby Gilbert
8. Muffin Spencer-Devlin
9. Fuzzy Zoeller
10. Jacky Cupit
11. Tommy Valentine
12. Davis Love III
13. Mason Rudolph
14. Dudley Wysong
15. Kermit Zarley

© Bob Thomas Sports Photography

The
Golf
Courses

Yards and yards and yards of lush lawn is what camouflages the danger zones on golf courses. Poets believe golf courses are pastoral playgrounds because of the yards and yards and yards of lush lawn covering them. Poets are ignoramuses in this instance. Golf courses are plainly minefields. Ask any serious golfer, pro or amateur.

Yards of lush lawn can tempt the Casual Golfer, mislead the Casual Golfer. Golf courses everywhere are full of sand traps, water holes the breadth and depth of the Atlantic Ocean, and, oh yes, "Damn Trees"—the despicable variety of tree grown only on golf courses worldwide.

The gruesome description of golf courses presented in this chapter is not meant to dissuade anyone from attempting this demonic diversion. Just a warning.

See, golf courses everywhere can be as seductive as the game itself. Serious golfers daydream all the time about tramping up the eighteenth fairway at Augusta National—Masters victory and green jacket in hand. Then again, serious golfers always envision soaring shots blending sublimely with blue sky, and too often their dreams and golf balls land in a grove of Damn Trees.

What follows is a sampling of nineteen different, difficult, and amusing golf courses—all of them are potentially hazardous to your mental health and your supply of golf balls.

Left: *The elegant hotel at Banff Springs looks like the perfect sanctuary for frazzled golfers. The imposing northern pines surrounding this hole attract misguided shots. Locating the errant ball in such groves requires caddies with the tracking capabilities of radar.*

Public Courses
Banff Springs Hotel
Banff, Alberta

If scoring at Banff becomes unbearable, a golfer can always transform his or her putter into a walking stick and explore the exquisite terrain surrounding this stimulating Canadian course.

Great groves of northern pines line the fairways—and attract wayward golf balls and curious tourists. When golf balls fly off course, caddies with the tracking skills of Mounties are useful at Banff.

Nature, mountain wildlife, and man commingle tranquilly here. Friendly bears sometimes wander onto the course. Seeing deer and coyotes is more common at Banff than scoring eagles and birdies. Fearless, territorial elk often graze on the tall grass and occasionally barricade the fairways.

"We have about four hundred elk on the course," said Stan Bishop, the director of golf at Banff Springs Hotel. "They're born and bred here, so they don't leave to go into the mountains. We often see newborn calves."

Wilderness is part of the engaging charm of Banff, one more masterful Stanley Thompson course. The other part is the elegant scenery—the Rocky Mountains, the raging mountain torrent at the first tee of the Rundle Course. The magnificent vista can hypnotize golfers and dissolve their concentration, an almighty golfing commodity.

"I can't play Banff," Gene Sarazen, one of the finest golfers in history, once said. "The scenery won't permit me to concentrate."

Golfers who focus on the landscape instead of the course are apt to leave Banff sorrowfully. Defeating Banff, battling Banff even to a standoff, is impossible without attentiveness to the three tough layouts at Banff Springs, each of which is nine holes and christened for a nearby mountain —Tunnel, Rundle, and Sulphur.

"The Tunnel Course is a thinking man's course," Bishop said. "You have to play position golf."

The fourth hole at the Rundle Course, a 171-yard, par-3, is the signature hole at Banff because of its combination of beauty and treachery. The view from the tee dazzles and daunts golfers. The golfer gazes at Rundle Mountain and stares down at a green cut into the hillside. Weak tee shots are in jeopardy of sinking in a glacial lake.

The temptation at Banff is to linger in the tee box forever, so as to avoid spoiling the serenity and the setting with a shot of any kind.

Concord Hotel
Kiamesha Lake, New York

A golf course stretched on a rack may be one way to describe the "Monster" at the Concord.

"Joe Finger built it this way because no one ever goes out of their way to play an easy course," says Mike Castelluzzi, the director of golf. "It was set up to be an experience, not just a round of golf."

The Monster extends 7,966 yards from the monster tees, but shrinks to 7,471 yards from the championship tees. How lenient. How merciful. How does anyone survive? you ask.

Castelluzzi credits Finger with conceiving the colossal layout, but based on its unnerving dimensions, the designer could have been the "Marquis de Sod." In all, thirteen holes are 400 yards or longer, and three of the four par-3s exceed 200 yards, the longest measuring 248 yards.

Golfers gallant enough to play the two mammoth par-5s need hearty nerves and gigantic drives to avert mental meltdowns and, worse, a bogey or higher. The fourth hole is 632 yards from the monster tees and 610 yards from the championship tees. The green is not reachable in two, except with a grenade launcher, and, wouldn't you know it, the rigid rules of golf prohibit the use of artillery on courses.

"The design is as important as the length of the long holes," Castelluzzi says. "You can't get away with swinging out of your shoes. You have to be long and accurate."

Golfers who are long *and* accurate are as rare as repeat champions at the Masters. So the holes seem unreasonable, agreed?

The sixteenth hole at least is shorter than Number 4, but only fifty-four yards shorter from the monster tees. The green has never been reached in two, because a narrowing fairway and several sand traps protecting the green cause even golfers with exceptional strength to cringe and lay up.

"It's one of the best tests of golf in the East," Castelluzzi says.

The Monster is a test, all right. An endurance test. A stress test, too. Battling the Monster also gives golfers an excuse to spend the night in the hotel bar or the hotel itself, perhaps the owners' motives for building the dastardly course in the first place.

Cape Breton Highlands
Golf Links
Ingonish Beach, Nova Scotia

Average golfers usually spend plenty of time in the woods, either comforting small game struck by one of their misdirected shots, or visiting the burial ground of lost golf balls. So average golfers ought to feel comfortable and familiar with Cape Breton. The course unfolds near the ocean, then heads into the woods of Cape Breton National Park.

"Part of the course has lost its links character because we don't cut down the trees in the park," club pro Joe Robinson says. "Now it's a combination of seaside and woods."

There are more obstacles and scenery here besides water and woods. Grass mounds rise from and complicate many of the fairways. Golfers need a plan and accuracy to maneuver on such lumpy sod.

A round of golf at Cape Breton is an adventure on various terrains. There is the fun and daunting fourteenth hole known as "Tattie Bogle,"

Gaelic for "potato piles." There is not one flat surface on the way to the 545-yard hole.

The course and experience begin cruelly with two long par-4s. The first hole is 420 yards uphill. Golfers do not play the first hole as much as scale it.

The second hole is 445 yards from launching pad to green and bends right. An assortment of short holes and long holes, all seductive, all dangerous, all scenic, remain on the nature walk through the woods of Cape Breton, a Stanley Thompson design.

Doral Country Club
Miami, Florida

In 1960, the late Arthur Kaskel saw a golf resort where others saw swampland. Skepticism did not deter Kaskel. He bought the wasteland on the Everglades, anyway—a tract of land originally known as "Kaskel's Folly." Today, it is known as Doral, six golf courses built around a neighborhood of 650 luxury cottages.

"The idea of the resort being here seemed unfathomable at the time my grandfather bought the land," Bill Kaskel says. "It was just five miles west of the airport, but it was completely undeveloped. The perception was that this was the middle of nowhere, but time proved that a resort was a good idea."

Doral is sort of a golfer's Disneyland. Diversions other than golf entertain the guests and residents, but golf is the attraction. There are six courses on the property. The most famous and perilous of them is the Blue Course, designed by Dick Wilson and Bob van Hagge, and completed in 1962. Golfers often leave the course cursing the wiry Bermuda rough or grumbling about the head wind.

"Most people complain that they can't escape from the rough at all," says Terri Norris, an assistant pro. "They ask us how to do it. We just tell them to hit the ball on the fairway."

The horror hole on the course is the eighteenth, 437 dangerous yards long. The hole is hazardous to golf balls and leaders of the Doral Open,

because water borders the left side of the fairway, and second shots there somehow must carry over part of a lake. Landing on the green often does not mean success, either, because the putting surface slopes toward the waiting water. There is a long trap on the right side, too.

Serious golfers know the course as the "Blue Monster," but call it much worse in private.

Augusta National
Golf Club
Augusta, Georgia

Lucky professional golfers with invitations, and luckier spectators with admission badges, worship at the "Cathedral in the Pines" every April during the Masters. Teeing up in, or even just attending, the tournament at Bobby Jones's shrine and monument is for some a sort of religious experience. Augusta National is paradise…or hell, depending on what side of the restraining ropes you are walking on during the Masters.

Efflorescent azaleas and dogwood define the course and entrance the spectators; their presence and scent symbolize the beginning of spring to golfers in the same way the first pitch of the season represents renewal to rooters of baseball teams.

On the other hand, the pro golfers pursuing history and the gaudy green jacket the Masters' champion receives believe the azaleas, dogwood, and towering Georgia pines to be interference and intrusive impediments to their work and earning potential. The plant life at Augusta National is one element of its enchantment; the course is famous, too, because of its mythology and camouflaged treachery.

The prettiest and toughest holes on the course, the eleventh, twelfth, and thirteenth, form "Amen Corner." Pros regularly leave Amen Corner muttering obscenities rather than chanting hosannas.

"The regular guys with square grooves don't have much of a chance here," American pro Lanny Wadkins says. "This isn't a place where you hit it as far as you can. You have to invent shots, work the ball, think ahead, play the wind, use your imagination. When the wind blows here, you probably can narrow the field that can win to ten guys."

The twelfth hole at Augusta National Golf Club—the middle hole of unplayable, unimaginable Amen Corner.

Even a golf ball doesn't seem small enough to navigate through the narrow alley on the finishing hole at Augusta.

Harbour Town Golf Links Hilton Head, South Carolina

The most recognizable landmark at Harbour Town is the lighthouse that stands behind the eighteenth hole. Sadly, it is just an ornament. No beacon from the lighthouse helps golfers navigate this relatively short but deceptive course, where sidestepping stray alligators sunbathing in one of the bunkers is occasionally necessary.

Alligators, however, seldom come ashore at Harbour Town, but the procedure to follow in the event of a visit is covered in the list of local rules. Just in case you need to know what to do.

"You get a club's length relief from an alligator," says Cary Corbitt, the sports director for Sea Pines Plantation, a resort complex that includes Harbour Town.

The wildlife, it seems, is tamer than the layout.

"The greens here are difficult to get to," Corbitt says. "But if you reach them in regulation, you have a birdie opportunity. You have an opportunity to sink the putt. This is a shot maker's course."

This is a Pete Dye course, too. Dye designed Harbour Town, which opened in 1969, with assistance from Jack Nicklaus. The fairways are narrow, the greens are miniature, although flat, thankfully.

The identifiable holes on the course are the closing holes. The seventeenth, a par-3, plays into the Calibogue Sound. Beware: Calibogue is pronounced "Cali-bogey."

The eighteenth hole, 458 yards long, requires two squarely struck shots over marshlands and the sound. The green is surrounded by bunkers, but frightened golfers looking for help landing their golf ball safely on the putting surface are alone. The lighthouse behind them provides no help, no comfort, no beacon.

Pebble Beach Golf Links Pebble Beach, California

Golfers distrustful of their ability to accurately gauge the speed and direction of the wind ought to consider hiring a meteorologist *and* a caddie when playing a round at the renowned resort that uses the Pacific Ocean as its water hole. Sea breezes can change into gale-force winds anytime at Pebble Beach. Unforeseen zephyrs in the past were known to instantaneously change the course of golf balls and the Bing Crosby National Pro-Am.

Arnold Palmer was contending in the 1964 Crosby until his second shot at Number 14 struck a tree. He was expecting to make three or four, surely no more than par five.

Palmer made nine.

The following day, a gust felled the intrusive tree.

The course turns inland at Number 11, shielding golfers from that four-letter word. Wind. The seventeenth hole, a par-3, was essentially the finishing hole in two opens at Pebble Beach. In the 1972 Open, Jack Nicklaus's approach shot struck the flagstick, enabling him to birdie the hole and win the open. In 1982, Tom Watson defeated Nicklaus by sinking a miracle chip shot from the kind of ugly grass Lawn Doctor makes house calls to kill.

Good fortune, though, rarely displaces the baffling, relentless wind at Pebble Beach.

Above: *The imposing Pacific Ocean regularly swallows wayward approach shots hoping to land on the finishing hole at Pebble Beach Golf Links. Opposite page: What looks like the surface of the moon actually is the second green at St. Andrews Golf Club.*

St. Andrews Golf Club
Fife, Scotland

St. Andrews is the second-auldest course anywhere, and a historic trail leading to the origins of golf. Archaeologists someday may discover the remains of an ancient, inaccurate clan of golfers in the Elysian Fields; Hell Bunker, a deep and often inescapable pit at the fourteenth hole; the Beardies; the Swilken Burn, a wee brook that protects the first green and regularly drowns weak approach shots; the Valley of Sin, the lower level of the eighteenth green from where three putts

and four putts are common; or maybe the Road Bunker at the seventeenth hole.

"The more I studied the Old Course, the more I loved it, and the more I loved it, the more I studied it," Bobby Jones once said. "I came to feel that it was, for me, the most favorable meeting ground possible for an important contest." The course is full of peril, charm, and ancient history. Golf was officially born at St. Andrews in 1754.

"Winning a green jacket [the souvenir of Masters champions] is fabulous," says Englishman Nick Faldo, "but winning [the British Open] at St. Andrews, in this atmosphere, in this fabulous town, it's very special. It's every golfer's dream."

Faldo won the 1990 British Open with the second-lowest total in 119 opens, 270, and with the victory came immortality and position along-

side past open champions. St. Andrews is about Harry Vardon, Walter Hagen, Bobby Jones, Sam Snead, Ben Hogan, Peter Thomson, Bobby Locke, Jack Nicklaus. It is also about Old Tom Morris and Young Tom Morris, open titlists in 1861, 1862, 1865, 1867, 1868, 1869, 1870, and 1872.

St. Andrews is on the north side of an old university town, and its complex of four courses —Old, New, Eton, and Jubilee—resembles nothing more than a flat park.

What distinguishes St. Andrews from other public courses on Earth, indeed all courses on Earth, besides its age, is double greens on fourteen of the eighteen holes. Miscalculating golfers may end up facing putts as long as football fields. Miscalculating golfers may also end up lost in St. Andrews's heather and lore.

© Bob Thomas Sports Photography

Umbrellas are golfers' and spectators' shields from rain at Muirfield, but nothing can protect them from the wicked wind.

Muirfield
Gullane, Scotland

The holes at Muirfield do not have bleak, foreboding nicknames such as "Woe-be-Tide," the stage name of the fourth at Turnberry. The holes at Muirfield have no nicknames at all. They don't need them.

There is not a tree or a shrub on the fairway, either.

What Muirfield does have is more than 150 flat bunkers camouflaging the landing area and deceiving the golfers.

Muirfield is on the frothy Firth of Forth between Gullane and North Berwick, and is Jack Nicklaus's favorite Scottish course. He won the

1966 British Open there. Nicklaus enjoys the layout so much that he christened his golf club Muirfield Village.

When the British Open was played there in 1892, Muirfield was not the word most golfers were using to describe the course. One critic, Andra Kirkaldy, actually was more poetic than profane when he scornfully called Muirfield "nothing more than an auld water-meadie."

The fact that the field had been beaten by an amateur, Harold H. Hilton, probably was more responsible for the grumbling than the condition of the course.

Muirfield is an accommodating golf course. The fairways must not have been fed enough, because most of them are slim, but the lies are usually absolutely perfect.

There are long par-5s and short par-5s; short, curvaceous par-4s and long par-4s just a little wider than a parking space. The par-3s are short and treacherous or longer but reachable without reliance on USGA-disapproved, hand-held artillery.

The diabolical design of Muirfield—the outgoing nine goes clockwise, and the incoming nine circles counterclockwise—ensures an untoward wind on at least sixteen holes.

The vagaries of the wind either flatter or baffle the golfer teeing up at Muirfield. Jack Nicklaus was able to drive the fifteenth hole, all 407 yards, when he won the 1966 British Open. But he had to squeeze hard on a three-wood to reach the sixteenth hole, a hole almost half the length of the fifteenth.

Oakmont Country Club Oakmont, Pennsylvania

Johnny Miller left Oakmont two decades ago telling a tall tale instead of one more horror story. Miller shot a 63 in the final round of the 1973 U.S. Open and won his first major championship. A 63 in the open would be the golfing equivalent of a fish story, except the score is USGA and PGA approved. One significant detail is missing, however, according to an Oakmont employee.

"Not to take anything away from Johnny's score," caddie master Steve Matthews says, "because that's a great round under any condi-

tions. But that day, Oakmont wasn't Oakmont."

Dry, nasty Oakmont had shrunk overnight in rainwater. The result of the downpour was a soggy course, an easier course, and a birdie bonanza. Miller got even with par and the course because the greens were softer, and thus simpler to read and putt on in the fourth round of that open. Normal Oakmont greens are slicker than wet pavement. The greens seem impervious to moving golf balls.

"It's not uncommon to see a person above the hole with an eight-foot putt watch his or her ball roll twenty-two feet beyond the hole and completely off the green," Matthews says.

Henry Fownes initially designed the course in 1904, and his son, William, modified it several

times afterward. Traps of all configurations and sizes were William Fownes's fiendish contribution to the landscape. The infamous traps are the "Church Pews" on the third and fifteenth holes, a sinister series of hazards. The nickname ought to be "Death Row."

Traps were William Fownes's means of penalizing players strong enough to outdrive the original dimensions of the layout.

"We still keep the penal nature of the course intact today," club pro Bob Ford says. "As players outgrow the distance to the bunkers, we just move the traps."

Maintaining Oakmont as some sort of golfing penal institution apparently was William Fownes's wish and legacy.

© Fred Vuich/FPG International

Wayward golfers frequently congregate in the "Church Pews," the traps on the third and fifteenth holes at Oakmont Country Club. Saving par from them requires more than skill—often it requires a miracle.

Pine Valley Golf Club Clementon, New Jersey

"Pain" Valley ought to be the name of this course, because agony connects nearly all of the stories about Pine Valley.

"I don't want to remember too much some-times," says Charlie Raudenbush, the club pro. "I tend to block it out, because I have to go out there again."

Serious golfers rate Pine Valley the toughest course in the world, because rounds there usually produce an abundance of unreasonable and unplayable lies and unthinkable and unspeakable scores.

The grim nicknames of some of the hazards on the course ought to petrify even fearless golfers.

"Hell's Half Acre" aptly describes the gargantuan trap bisecting the first and second fairways of the seventh hole, an unbearably long par-5. Putts rolling toward the tenth hole have been known to drop off the green into a pit in front known as "Devil's Aperture." The fifth hole, an unnerving par-3, apparently was so difficult during the 1936 Walker Cup match that opponents Jack McLean of Scotland and Charlie Yates of Georgia co-wrote a poem about their experience. Their six lines of doggerel constitute a typical Pine Valley horror story:

We think that we shall never see,
A tougher course than Pine Valley.
Trees and traps wherever we go
And clumps of earth flying through the air.
This course was made for you and me.
But only God can make a THREE.

Pine Valley is an equally intimidating and inviting golf course. Nobody, it seems, wants to play at Pine Valley. But then again, everybody wants to play at Pine Valley. Jack Nicklaus was nearby and reportedly interrupted his honeymoon more than thirty years ago to challenge his skills and the sandy layout. For better or worse, he shot a score of 74 on the course.

© Bob Thomas Sports Photography

"Everybody has fun here," Raudenbush says. "They take the attitude that it's a golf mecca and respect it on that basis. Big numbers will happen because at some point you're going to wind up with an unplayable lie. It's that kind of place."

Royal St. George's Golf Club Sandwich, England

In 1985, the last time the British Open was held at Royal St. George's, the serpent's breath known meekly as wind blew strong enough to whisk Jack Nicklaus out of the tournament. Nicklaus shot 77 and 75 the first two rounds and did not survive the cut for the first time since his first open in 1962.

There were playable conditions in the after-noon: meaning it was just windy. In the morning, when Nicklaus played, it was very, very windy.

Sandy Lyle went on to win the tournament —how appropriate, because the amount of sand at Royal St. George's matches the amount of wind at Royal St. George's, a true links course on the coast of the English Channel.

The fairways are full of gorse and monstrous grassy moguls, and the course is full of traps the width and depth of moon craters—the result of nature, with help, doubtlessly, from irritated golfers excavating deeper and deeper to extricate their unfortunate golf balls.

There is apparently enough sand on the third hole alone to cover an entire desert. How else to explain its ominous nickname, "Sahara?"

How unsporting is Royal St. George's? Nicklaus was nine over par when he won the St. George's Challenge Cup in 1959, and members at the time thought his two-round total of 149 was bloody good, indeed.

Royal Troon
Ayrshire, Scotland

Opposite page: The fairways at Royal St. George's are full of grassy moguls, gorse, and traps the breadth and depth of moon craters. Below: The eighth hole at Royal Troon, the horrific Postage Stamp, is the shortest, but also one of the hardest, holes in British championship golf.

Transportation home from "Hell" is easier to obtain than a par at Royal Troon—a railway runs outside the rough on the eleventh fairway, and an international airport is nearby. Fleeing Troon, a links course on the west coast of Scotland, is often wiser than testing Troon.

Oh, yes, Arnold Palmer shot 276 there in 1962, and the grand prize was his second consec-

utive British Open title. But grim tales, unspeakable horror stories unimaginable even by the novelist Stephen King, greatly outnumber happy endings at Troon. In 1950, German amateur Hermann Tissies struck his golf ball into all three traps protecting the eighth green—the "Postage Stamp," and the smallest and shortest hole in British championship golf. The distance to the green from the tee is 126 yards. But Tissies took fifteen there, needing five swipes to escape from one of the bunkers.

Legend and amateur alike have been licked by the Postage Stamp. In the 1923 British Open,

© FPG International

dapper Walter Hagen made an ugly double bogey there and wound up one shot behind the champion, Arthur Havers. In 1962, Jack Nicklaus sank a putt from fifty feet on the eleventh hole, a par-5, 481 yards long.

This was a bad thing?

Well, the surprise ending to this short story is the putt was for a ten on the hole. Nicklaus was strong and young then, and apparently unfamiliar with Latin and the motto of the course: *Tam arte quam marte.* In English: As much by skill as by strength. He attacked the fairway with a driver and really could have used a machete to hack back onto the short grass from the tall, wiry whin.

Palmer won the tournament at the eleventh, scoring two eagles and two birdies there by using his mind, a one-iron from the tee, and a two-iron to the green.

Shinnecock Hills Golf Club Southampton, New York

North Sea, the sign reads on the road to magnificent and imposing Shinnecock Hills. You chuckle, but not convincingly, even though you are certain you are thousands of miles from Great Britain and the European mainland, which *the* North Sea bisects. This North Sea is on Long Island.

Yet, driving slowly through the dense fog that shrouds Route 27, you can imagine heading down the coast of England—perhaps toward Royal St. George's in Sandwich, England, the European links course Shinnecock Hills is said to most resemble.

Shinnecock Hills is not an authentic links course because it is too far inland and does not exactly touch water. Shinnecock Hills, though, is the best American facsimile.

It is open, and the few trees on the course often are immaterial during rounds. Shinnecock Hills is also a scrubby course, a heathland course.

The Indian grass that lines much of the fairways generally stands a foot or taller. Beyond the grass lurk the fragrant but treacherous beach plum and bayberry bushes—sinister shrubbery, indeed. The thorny beach plum and bayberry bushes prick the fingers, legs, and psyche of the golfer misfortunate and inaccurate enough to land in them.

The one significant similarity between Shinnecock Hills and the links courses of Scotland and England is the wind, which whips off the Atlantic Ocean and Peconic Bay daily and threatens to launch golfers and their golf balls into orbit.

Turnberry (Ailsa Course) Ayrshire, Scotland

Turnberry is full of Scottish enchantment, unidentifiable rough that is easy to land in but nearly impossible to escape from, and dazzling landmarks—among them Ailsa Craig, a gigantic rock island, and namesake of the course that rises impressively from the sea.

Golf at Turnberry is auld-fashioned Scottish golf: low shots flying beneath high winds and prayers for a favorable bounce on dangerous greens. On unusual afternoons, when the wind is docile and the sky is baby blue instead of dress gray, Turnberry can be about slack flags, stiff shots, and low scores.

On normal afternoons there, panting winds cause the flags to sway, even solid shots to stray, and scores to rise even higher than the waves and the tide on the Firth of Clyde.

The two Turnberrys were visible during the 1977 British Open, and the open nine years later. Someone accidentally unplugged the wind machine in 1977. How else to explain the sublime conditions when Tom Watson barely outshot Jack Nicklaus in what experts believe was the most magnificent duel in the history of major championships?

Watson and Nicklaus went head to head and nearly shot for shot over the last thirty-six holes.

Watson shot 65 in the third round, and 65 in the fourth round. Nicklaus shot 65 in the third round, and 66 in the fourth round.

Difficult to believe, but neither Watson nor Nicklaus can claim to have shot the best round of golf ever at Turnberry. The honor belongs to Greg Norman, who, in standard Turnberry weather, somehow shot 63 in the second round of the 1986 Open, matching the course record, the tournament record, and the scoring record of all four major championships.

More incredible than the achievement was his reaction to the score: Norman was upset. "I was trying to shoot sixty."

Norman easily won the tournament, but only fought tough Turnberry to a stalemate.

Winged Foot Golf Club Mamaroneck, New York

Winged Foot is a golf curse, and no, the letter *o* was not omitted from the preceding word. "Curse" is a fairly accurate description of Winged Foot. The course is so arduous that even professional golfers were unable to solve the confounding layout until 1984, the year Fuzzy Zoeller easily won the fourth U.S. Open at Winged Foot with a 67 in a play-off against Greg Norman.

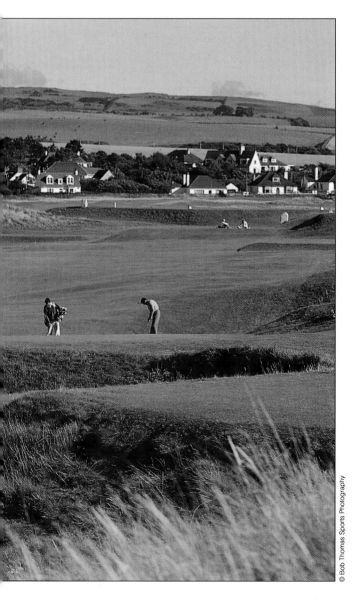

"You don't need rough on this course," Jack Nicklaus has said, "because the trees are bad enough. The trees put you in double jeopardy. The trees are so big they really define this course. There are so many of them, they narrow the fairways even more, and the fairways are not wide at all. It's simple: If you're in the trees at Winged Foot, you're in trouble."

Roget can dispute this claim, but trouble and Winged Foot are synonyms.

Tom Nieporte, now the club pro, remembers his introduction to Winged Foot, indeed his indoctrination to Winged Foot. It was one month prior to the 1959 U.S. Open, and Nieporte industriously read newspaper stories about the course. The contents, embellished somewhat here, were alarming:

The rough was so tall, golfers would require scythes to hack balls back onto the fairway.

Petrifying details of holes fifteen through eighteen, a series of oppressively difficult par-4s the members christened "Death Valley" years ago, awaited unsuspecting golfers.

"The stories were intimidating," Nieporte says. "By the time you arrived, you were afraid to play the course."

Winged Foot was created from the deliberately devious design of master architect A. W. Tillinghast, who was told to build a "man-sized course." The layout has been modified some since then, especially the tenth hole, a par-3 and the toughest hole on the course until the green was elevated and partially flattened before the 1974 U.S. Open. A house standing across from the tee caused Ben Hogan to describe the hole as a "three-iron to some guy's bedroom." Tillinghast was pleased with the original hole—according to him the best par-3 he ever designed—because an approach shot landing anywhere other than the center of the cruelly pitched green would carom into the rough beyond.

Golfers laying one on the original green were in position to brag, but possibly in position for disaster, too.

"If you were above the pin, God knows where you'd end up when you putted down," caddie master Pat Collins says.

The course nowadays is gentler than Tillinghast planned, but Winged Foot is still a curse.

Left: Wind and the whin usually complicate rounds of golf at Turnberry Golf Club. Above: Winged Foot is tamer than its designer, A. W. Tillinghast, planned, but the course frequently snarls at its quarry.

Courtesy Aberdeen Golf and Country Club

Unusual Courses

Aberdeen Golf and Country Club Boynton Beach, Florida

It is possible to shoot at a mermaid every day of the golf season on the eleventh hole of Aberdeen. The supernatural and the downright unimaginable is commonplace there, because the course was designed by Desmond Muirhead, the Salvador Dali of golf architects. Several of his courses are abounding with surreal imagery. The "Mermaid" is his most famous and fun hole.

"You can't appreciate what Desmond was trying to get across until you see it from the air," says Mike Farmer, the professional at the private club. "You can see a lot of the symbols when you're standing on the course, but you really can't see the navel until you're above it."

The complete shape of the Mermaid is indistinct from ground level, but from above its anatomy is noticeable, and uncannily recognizable. Two tee boxes serve as the tail fins. Patches of rough on the curvaceous fairway represent the scaly torso. A depression in the center of a fairway mound…well, that is the navel. The green is the head, and two sweeping sand traps behind it create the impression of blond tresses.

"When I got here," Farmer says, "I heard some of the holes were symbolic, but I never imagined teeing off from the tail of a mermaid."

"Beauty and the Beast," the nickname of hole Number 4, is more proof of Muirhead's playfulness, imagination, and inventiveness. Beauty and the Beast, 608 yards long, challenges the bravery and accuracy of golfers. The golfer can either launch his or her tee shot left toward a narrow fairway full of traps (the Beast), or drive 200 yards

Courtesy Aberdeen Golf and Country Club

Opposite page: *Mermaids do exist: The eleventh hole at Aberdeen Golf and Country Club is proof. Above: Aberdeen is full of quirky, surreal holes—the result of the imagination of Desmond Muirhead, the Salvador Dali of golf architects.*

across water to the comely island fairway on the right (Beauty).

Aberdeen is part golf course, part amusement park. The pleasure continues at Number 8: the "Dragon" hole. The twisting fairway is the neck, the green is the head, and a strip of bunker symbolizes flames. Patches of fairway and rough form the "Big Dipper" and "Little Dipper" at Number 12. Even more fun, in the shape of Marilyn Monroe, awaits golfers at Number 15.

Mount Massive Golf Club Leadville, Colorado

Golfers at Mount Massive ought to consider stowing one unconventional piece of equipment in their bags: an oxygen mask. The use of carts is impermissible at Mount Massive, so, because of all the walking necessary, lowlanders may have some trouble adapting their breathing patterns to golf at 9,700 feet.

"People from the flatlands usually play just once around," says the manager of the course, Joyce Pedersen. "Older people find it difficult [to finish]."

Mount Massive is the highest golf course in North America. The altitude leaves some golfers breathless, so does the extra-long distance their golf balls travel. The thin mountain air enables a golf ball to fly farther and average golfers to imitate Greg Norman or Fred Couples.

"I've played with a lot of golfers here who didn't realize how far the ball would go," Pedersen says. "It happens all the time. You get maybe fifteen percent more distance here than you get at sea level."

Egos expand along with the length of shots at Mount Massive, a nine-hole public course. The atmosphere can transform weaklings into power hitters. An expert golfer Pedersen knows regularly lands his drive on the fifth green, a distance of 318 yards from launching pad to green.

"Not everyone can expect to do that," Pederson says.

Double Eagle Golf Club Eagle Bend, Minnesota

Double Eagle is two different public courses on the same plot of land. It has nine holes and eighteen tees, the ingenious concept of its architect, Joel Goldstrand. The club's owner, Ron Weibye, says Double Eagle is the only reversible golf course in the United States (one recently was built in Japan).

"Joel had wanted to make a reversible golf course for some time, but he had never found the right piece of ground," Weibye says. "The elevations have to be correct, so that there aren't any blind shots when you reverse the course. You don't want a downhill par-3 to become an uphill par-3 with a blind shot.

"When he told me he wanted to do this here, I was really excited. I couldn't imagine why

Courtesy Double Eagle Golf Club

Laurens Golf and Country Club
Laurens, Iowa

The local golf course doubles as the local airport in Laurens, Iowa, so occasionally the runway on the eighth hole is busier than the fairway on the eighth hole.

"We sometimes go three or four days without having a plane land," says Zola Cresnek, the manager of the course. "But during crop-dusting season, in the spring and fall, sometimes they land every twenty minutes."

The semi-private golf course and airport have shared the same piece of property since 1957, when the founders of the airport, as a means of earning cash to offset declining air traffic, leased the land to the founders of the country club. Coexistence has been easy because pilots and golfers generally obey the most important local rule: Airplanes have the right of way. Small corporate and crop-dusting planes preparing to land are supposed to circle and buzz the course before descending. Golfers in the flight path then must yield to them.

"Some people get the wrong idea," says club member Dan Kendall. "When they think of an airport, they think of concrete runways. The runway here is grass."

The runway begins in the rough alongside the long eighth hole. Planes landing in Laurens cross over the fairway, touch down to the right of the eighth tee, and then continue south to the fourth fairway.

Pilots unfamiliar with the airport and its quirky landing procedure have been known to go off course and onto more of the course than intended.

A foursome of women walked up to the eighth green not too long ago only to discover an unusual obstacle between their golf balls and the cup—an airplane. The pilot had missed the runway. In this case, pilot error did not hurt anyone, but the greens keeper did have to repair some uncommonly large divots.

Above: Golf junkies need at least two full days of play to satiate their habit at Double Eagle, a reversible golf course. Opposite page: Playing golf makes Clint Eastwood's day.

more courses didn't do it, especially in rural areas where it doesn't pay to build a regular eighteen-hole golf course."

Golf was an unfamiliar sport to residents of Eagle Bend before Weibye built his dream course. Introducing Minnesotans to an outdoor sport other than fishing was part of his plan, though initially Weibye did have to use a lure, in this case a supper club, to hook his neighbors on golf. Today, Double Eagle has 250 members.

Golf junkies need at least two days to fully indulge their habit at Double Eagle. The Gold layout is open on even-numbered days of each month, and the Green layout is playable on the odd days. Gold benches, gold ball washers, and gold signs identify the Gold Course. The color coding helps prevent one of the potential hazards of reversible golf: someone inadvertently golfing the wrong way on a two-way fairway.

ARCTIC GOLF

■

The seven hundred or so members of High Country Club shout "brrrrr" and "fore" during their rounds of golf.

High Country is the coldest course on Earth.

It is four hundred miles from the Arctic Circle on the shores of the Beaufort Sea in northern Canada. The course has nine holes and sand greens and was founded in 1975 by missionary Dave Freeman.

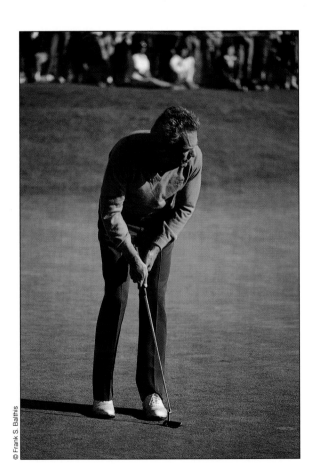

© Frank S. Balthis

"WHY I LIKE GOLF:"

■

JOHNNY BENCH

Baseball Hall of Fame catcher

"I like getting away for four hours, away from everybody and everything. It's easier than catching, but there's nothing easy about finding my ball."

HANK KETCHAM

Cartoonist/creator of "Dennis The Menace"

"You don't go home and talk about the great tennis courts that you played, but you do talk about the great golf courses you played."

FRANK VIOLA

New York Mets pitcher

"I can get up and pitch in front of 55,000 people and not be nervous, because I know what I'm doing. On the golf course, I'm like a little kid again. I shake if cameras are on."

JAMES GARNER

Actor

"Probably the most exacting game that I know, the most difficult game to play well. I like it. You get away from business and think of nothing else."

CLINT EASTWOOD

Actor

"I couldn't tell you what exactly I like about golf. It's a nice game, but a little masochistic. Just when you think you've got it mastered, it lets you know that you haven't."

KATHY WHITWORTH

Professional golfer/member of LPGA Hall of Fame

"You're not going to hit the ball perfectly all the time. You have some bad holes and make some mental errors, and you're distraught about that. But at least you know you can put a few shots together and you might get a few birdies coming in to salvage something."

MARK McGWIRE

Oakland Athletics first baseman

"I like golf because when the marshal tells the gallery to be quiet, it gets quiet. Try that in baseball, the crowd gets louder."

LEE TREVINO

Professional golfer

"One of the reasons I love it is that nobody has ever mastered it, and nobody ever will. Jack Nicklaus has come the closest. If you put it on a scale of 100, he got up there about 97, and everybody else was at about 40."

The Toughest Holes

Golf is an equal romance between player(s) and landscape…until a round begins, and the domineering landscape begins to control the relationship, mocking its suitor(s) until their rendezvous ends.

Golfers seldom leave courses completely happy, but golfers usually return. *Oddball* is another word meaning "golfer." Golfers hate to love the game. Golfers love to hate the game, because most golfers cannot actually play the game. Golfers cannot give up the game, either. Golfers dread stepping up to the first tee. Golfers anticipate arriving at the first tee. "Someone help me, someone stop me," golfers ought to plead before addressing the golf ball. Golfers are incapable of controlling their habit or of surviving without the game. In fact, there are some people who view it as an addiction.

This ought to make you happy that you are a reader instead of a golfer…at least for today. What follows is a tour of eighteen of the toughest golf holes in the world—in convenient book form. What this entitles you to is all the fun, minus the aggravation, lost golf balls, and a therapy bill.

But before you begin playing this dream/nightmare course in your imagination, please recite silently, reflexively, from this standard mental checklist:

"Waggle once. Waggle twice. Waggle three times. Head down. Knees bent. Head down. Distribute weight evenly on the balls of your feet. Head down. Ease up on the grip. Do not strangle the club. Yet. Head down. Concentrate. CONCENTRATE! Stiffen your left arm. Slacken your right arm. Head down. Alert the search party to peer right," the normal flight path of tee shots.

Number 13 at Augusta National Golf Club
465 yards, par-5

Dredging the creek that bisects the fairway and green of Number 13 at Augusta would probably provide enough golf balls to supply the Masters' field and the Masters' gallery for a year. The golf balls and hopes of countless prospective Masters champions lie on the bottom of the wicked water hole.

The thirteenth is an unusual par-5, because par-5s normally are 475 yards or longer. The thir-

teenth is also an unbelievably difficult par-5, in spite of its arithmetic inadequacy.

The fairway bends sharply left, and golfers whose tee shots land short of the dogleg ought not challenge the pitiless creek. Laying up is the cautious, but smart, strategy. Better to be safe than soggy.

There ought to be grave markers along the fairway commemorating the golfers whose

dreams of fame and immortality died at Number 13. There have been so many of them in Masters history, there will be more.

Tsuneyuki (Tommy) Nakajima of Japan once took thirteen strokes here. In 1937, Ralph Guldahl took six and wound up two shots behind the winner, Byron Nelson, who made three.

The casualty list is longer at the thirteenth than the distance to the green from the tee box.

Number 4 at Baltusrol Golf Club (Lower Course) Springfield, New Jersey
196 yards, par-3

A flapping white flag approximately 200 yards ahead is the target the good golfers shoot at when pulling the trigger on the fourth hole at Baltusrol.

So how about the bad golfers, you ask? What should all the bad golfers do at Number 4, an unnerving par-3? Well, the bad golfers, like the good golfers, ought to peer at the white flag from the tee box, but then retreat, heed its symbolism, and surrender.

Hitting onward endangers the bad golfer, places him or her in jeopardy of losing a golf ball or two…or three…or four, plus all confidence and mental faculties.

The approach to the hole is uncomplicated: You whack a golf ball until it clears the huge moat protecting the wide green with two tiers. Reaching the green, though, is difficult: Water drowns weak shots, and bunkers alongside and behind the green collect imprecise and muscle-bound shots.

Golf course architect Robert Trent Jones is the person to credit and/or blame for the hole. He modified the layout prior to the 1954 U.S. Open. Jones's dynamic response to criticism of his revisions was to tee up a ball, launch it toward the hole, and watch it submerge in the cup.

Number 18 at Bay Hill Club Orlando, Florida
441 yards, par-4

Opposite page: Beware! The casualty list is even longer at the thirteenth hole of Augusta National than the distance from the tee to the green.

The lake surrounding the finishing hole here is a source of frustration for golfers, and a source of income for the scuba diver who every two weeks plunges into the water, gathers a multitude of sunken golf balls, and then sells them.

Professionals and amateurs alike help enrich the scuba diver. Mishits from exceptional golfers and average golfers supply the scuba diver with plenty of work and money.

The scuba diver may have been working overtime in 1989. The eighteenth hole at Bay Hill was the horror hole on the PGA Tour that year, according to the official PGA media guide. The stroke average there during the Nestle Invitational was 4.559, the result, doubtlessly, of too many long approach shots landing short of the boomerang-shaped green and in the scuba diver's vault.

Splash! and unprintable words, it seems, are familiar sounds at the eighteenth. The golfing gods, though, do not seize and sink every shot soaring above their pool. In 1990, poor ol' rich Greg Norman lost one more tournament, unbelievably, when rookie Robert Gamez sank his approach shot from 170 yards to beat Norman in the Nestle Invitational.

Number 17 at Cypress Point Golf Club
Pebble Beach, California
371 yards, par-4

The tee box here provides golfers shelter and the best view of a spectacularly beautiful seascape.

So, squeezing the trigger at Number 17 is difficult because: (1) the magnificent topography of the coastline hypnotizes people and (2) errant golf shots invariably crash-land in the imposing Pacific Ocean or bound off sinister rock formations.

The combination of appreciation of the exquisite setting and apprehension of the trial ahead make lingering safely in the tee box an understandable preference to chancing the hole, and fate. Sooner or later, though, the golfer has to recover from the topographical spell, or overcome his or her psychological paralysis and address the tee shot. But with what club? A howling head wind is the prevailing wind, so there are times when a driver is too weak a weapon to launch the ball sufficiently right down the fairway.

A cluster of gnarled cypress trees rising sadistically from the center of the fairway further complicates the hole. Gallant or foolish is the golfer who takes the right-hand route over the Pacific Ocean to the hole. The golf ball just may disappear into the waves.

Sandy Tatum, past president of the USGA, calls Cypress Point "the Sistine Chapel of golf."

You can call it Hell.

© Stephen Dunn/Allsport

Opposite page: Sandy Tatum, past president of the USGA, calls Number 17 at Cypress Point Golf Club, "the Sistine Chapel of Golf." You may wish to substitute Sinister for Sistine. Above: Robert Trent Jones is one of the most famous and fiendish golf course architects of all time.

GOLF COURSE ARCHITECTURE

Golf usually is an uphill, downhill battle between the golfer, nature, landscape, and the true enemy: the fiendish golf course architect. Golf course architects insist their creations are meant to challenge golfers of all levels of ability, especially average golfers with handicaps ranging from twelve to twenty-six.

The most flamboyant golf course architects in history, such as Robert Trent Jones, Albert Warren Tillinghast, Stanley Thompson, Alister McKenzie, Desmond Muirhead, Donald Ross, and Pete Dye, include aspects of their personalities in their designs—apparently most of them have small, diabolical, sadistic streaks.

The toughest courses are full of humps, bumps, and bunkers, slopes and swales, treacherous islands, railroad ties, and trouble, plenty of trouble. Architects claim to be innocent traditionalists, upholders of an ancient game. Terrible golfers ought to blame the originators of golf, the Scots and English, the architects declare.

"As we are indebted to the Scots for our principles of the game," Robert Trent Jones once wrote, "so are we indebted to them for our principles of architecture...a strategic theory implicit in the best British courses."

Golf course architecture is different nowadays, though no more lenient. Professional golfers such as Jack Nicklaus, Arnold Palmer, Gary Player, and architects such as Bob van Hagge are real estate developers as well as designers. These men are creating neighborhoods around almost every one of their golf holes. They are modifying the characteristics of the fairways to suit the needs of the builders.

"Most new courses wouldn't be built if they weren't tied to real estate," says van Hagge, who helped Dick Wilson design Doral Country Club from swampland more than twenty-five years ago. "Golf courses are being built these days to sell real estate."

Number 16 at Firestone Country Club
Akron, Ohio
625 yards, par-5

Hell has bunkers on the right…water troughs on the right…a lake in the middle…an assortment of vile trees on either side…and a name: the sixteenth at Firestone.

Number 16 is a serpent that snakes 625 yards, and few golfers can defeat it without possessing valor, strength, and probably Jack Nicklaus's jumbo driver.

The pros refer to Number 16 as "the Monster." No explanation necessary, agreed?

The path leading to the hole bends left, the optimum direction of the tee shot. Golf balls heading right, face the likelihood of landing in one of the two strategic and vexing bunkers guarding the edge of a fairway that slopes toward the left. Reaching the green in two is not impossible, but the attempt is inadvisable. Third shots sometimes are not safe from the intimidating lake defending the front of the green.

Arnold Palmer was charging toward the World Series of Golf championship in 1962 until his third shot sank. He was thinking four, but left the green scratching an eight onto his card.

Sam Snead, at the age of fifty-four, lost his golf ball and also his bid to win the 1966 PGA Championship in the lousy drink at Number 16.

Number 13 at Medinah Country Club (Number 3)
Medinah, Illinois
219 yards, par-3

Medinah, according to local history, originally was going to be an obliging tract of gracious sod; a playful, playable layout, indeed; "a sporty little course that will become famous the country over to and for women."

But Medinah grew up mean, became too long and too ornery for most women, and nowadays is too long and too ornery for most men.

There are eighteen examples of nastiness at Medinah Number 3, the thirteenth hole is merely one of them.

Landing anywhere near the hole requires good aim, good fortune, and mostly the courage and strength to challenge and clear Lake Kadijah, guardian of the sloping green. A bunker on the golfers' right also complicates the approach shot.

Number 13 was equally troublesome when, before revisions to the course, it was the seventeenth hole.

Clayton Heafner and Sam Snead were chasing Cary Middlecoff in the 1949 U.S. Open at Medinah before each bogeyed the seventeenth during the fourth round. Their misfortune enabled Middlecoff to win the championship by a shot.

In the 1975 U.S. Open, two pars, two average scores, would have enabled Ben Crenshaw to overtake John Mahaffey and Lou Graham. But his approach shot to Number 17 was weak and, worse, wound up wet. Crenshaw made double bogey, and Graham became one of the unlikeliest open champions in history by defeating Mahaffey in a play-off.

Opposite page: *Landing anywhere near the thirteenth hole at Medinah Number 3 requires remarkable aim, terrific luck, and the valor to challenge and the strength to clear Lake Kadijah, guardian of the sloping green.*

Number 5 at Oakland Hills Country Club Birmingham, Michigan
405 yards, par-4

Donald Ross said the Great Golf Course Developer in the Sky beckoned him to build Oakland Hills.

"The Lord intended this for a golf course," Ross said when he originally saw the land the country club occupies these days. It seemed to be perfectly suited to the game.

So Ross built a golf course, a good golf course.

Then Robert Trent Jones created a "monster," according to one of the professional golfing gods, Ben Hogan. Jones added fifty booby traps to the layout prior to the 1951 U.S. Open.

Hogan shot 67 in the fourth round and won the tournament (his third of four open titles), but he left the course grumbling, anyway. Pro golfers despise sand traps—often hazardous to the size of their paycheck and all that.

T. C. Chen of China was going to defeat Andy North and slay the Monster, too, until he came to the fifth hole during the final round of the 1985 U.S. Open. The creek bisecting the fifth fairway 280 yards from the tee did not bother him. The unbearably deep rough at Number 5 did Chen in.

He was comfortably ahead of North until his second shot landed in what the USGA calls open rough, and what pros scornfully call "that deep green stuff."

Chen chipped from the green stuff, the ball struck the club face twice, and he wound up with a penalty and an eight. North made birdie, made up five shots on one hole, and won by a stroke.

Number 15 at Oakmont Country Club
Oakmont, Pennsylvania
453 yards, par-4

What caliper best measures the difficulty of the fifteenth at Oakmont? Ben Hogan was unable to conquer the hole. He made six and five there in the last two rounds of the 1953 U.S. Open. Hogan won the championship easily, but the fifteenth hole beat him.

The uphill tee shot here must ascend the long rise of fairway leading to a narrow landing area full of danger: "Church Pew" bunkers on the left and normal bunkers and ditches on the right. The fairway then slopes gently toward an enormous putting surface squeezed by bunkers, the longest extending almost the length of a football field, one hundred yards.

Correctly judging and negotiating the distance to the hole from the fairway is vital, because miscalculation can lead to catastrophe. In golf terms: bogey, double bogey, triple bogey, etc.

When Johnny Miller shot 63 in the final round of the 1973 U.S. Open and left the course with a tournament record and the title in hand, he played Number 15 perfectly. His secret: a magical driver, a magical four-iron, and one putt from ten feet.

It can be that easy at Oakmont.

But not often.

Number 16 at Olympic Club
San Francisco, California
604 yards, par-5

The U.S. Supreme Court ought to examine the constitutionality of the sixteenth at Olympic. A hole tough enough to frazzle Ben Hogan and Arnold Palmer cannot be legal.

Golfing gods expect to make four at such holes, and surely no more than five. But Hogan, chasing his fifth title, and Palmer, pursuing his second championship, made uncharacteristic errors and sixes in separate opens at Number 16 and wound up losing play-offs.

Birdies at Number 15 and Number 18 put nondescript Jack Fleck in position to tie Hogan at the end of regulation in the 1955 U.S. Open. The par Fleck made at Number 16 was as improbable as it was significant, since he drove his golf ball into the thick fairway rough.

In 1966, Palmer was seven shots ahead of Billy Casper, with nine holes remaining in the tournament. Inscribing his name on the trophy was a mere formality, since Arnold appeared to be the winner-to-be.

Declaring Palmer the champion was premature, because he and Casper left the sixteenth sharing first place when Palmer made bogey and Casper made birdie. Casper won the play-off by four shots.

A shrunken fairway that bends left complicates the tee shot. Proper placement is vital on this hole, because clusters of indiscriminate trees and bunkers left and right of the green coldly confiscate the golf balls of inexact golfers of average and legendary ability.

Opposite page: *The seventh hole at Pebble Beach Golf Links, the shortest hole in American championship golf, is full of water, trouble, and traps.*

Number 7 at Pebble Beach Golf Links
Pebble Beach, California
107 yards, par-3

Wind velocity and direction determine the severity or simplicity of the seventh hole at Pebble Beach Golf Links in sunny California—107 yards of unpredictability.

"If the wind is gusting in your face, it's like a two-hundred-yard shot," says R. J. Harper, the course professional. "It's a fairly simple hole when it's calm."

Number 7 seldom is simple, using the one accurate barometer here, that being Pebble Beach history.

It was so windy during the Bing Crosby Clambake one year, pro Art Wall unsheathed his putter to attack the green. He cleverly stroked the golf ball downhill toward the hole, and while it landed in a green-side bunker, Wall made par anyway. The goal, agreed?

"He just wanted to keep the ball low and in play," Harper says.

Imagination and patience sometimes are as important as proper club selection at the seventh hole. Approach shots struck too solidly on the

shortest hole in championship golf may descend into the largest water hole on Earth. The Pacific Ocean.

The seventh is a treacherously beautiful blending of sand and seascape: There are more than enough bunkers protecting the miniature green. Exactly six too many.

Too much sand and surf and way too little turf on the putting surface complicate the seventh at Pebble Beach, one of the most challenging and interesting holes in golf.

© Frank S. Balthis

The unusual bunker in the middle of the green taunts and often ambushes the greedy golfers leaving the sixth hole at Riviera Country Club.

Number 2 at Pine Valley
Clementon, New Jersey
367 yards, par-4

Pine Valley looks more like a golf corpse, because all sorts of dead areas predominate patches of emerald grass.

Pine Valley, full of insufferable shrubbery and ugly underbrush, is the antithesis of the modern immaculate golf course, where, it seems, each blade of grass receives individual care from the greens keeper.

The toughest course in the world—its universal reputation—is actually one enormous wasteland in the New Jersey wilderness.

The second hole typifies Pine Valley. The fairway is a slim chute, and there is a series of dangerous bunkers on the right side and several pot bunkers on the left side.

Reaching the green requires crossing a wasteland of scrub pines, Scottish broom, and sand. Footprints are evidence of unfortunate golfers who have gone before on the treacherous terrain, and those same footprints are also reminders of the necessity of landing on the fairway.

"Pine Valley is not tough," Arnold Palmer is said to have declared, presumably through a grin wider than some of the fairways there.

"As long as you can hit the ball straight, keep it out of sand, and putt reasonably well."

Golfers attacking Pine Valley with all three of those almighty golfing weapons are rarer there than rounds below 70.

Number 6 at Riviera Country Club
Pacific Palisades, California
160 yards, par-3

Club members sizing up the sixth hole at Riviera usually stand above their tee shots with birdie on their minds, then typically walk off the green muttering and entering bogeys, or worse, on their scorecards.

The bunker in the middle of the green mocks the greedy golfers leaving the hole.

The bunker in the middle of the green? Yes, the bunker in the middle of the green.

Number 6 is known as the novel bunker to outsiders. It's *@#*&* bunker to most club members.

"They're not too happy with it," assistant pro Gordon Krah says. "Sometimes, depending on the pin placement, you can hit a shot ten feet to the right of the pin and be in the bunker. A lot of people have mixed feelings about the bunker. Some people like it because it's one of a kind. A lot of people don't think it's worth it because sometimes you get penalized for hitting a good shot."

Gimmicks are rarities at Riviera, where accurate driving often produces low scores.

Club members are prosperous people, so perhaps the purpose of the bunker on the sixth hole is to reemphasize to them that golf and life often are unsporting, and to use a sand wedge as a walking stick when approaching the green.

Number 12 at Royal Birkdale
Lancashire, England
190 yards, par-3

The captivating and dangerous links-course botany and the wicked wind off the Irish Sea are the enemies at this hole.

Land in the gorse, whin, bracken, or broom, and chances are teams of Englishmen with weed whackers will be unable to recover the missing ball.

Royal Birkdale is made from typical British Open terrain—imposing sandhills, clumps of tortuous heather, mountainous grassy moguls that resemble the Himalayas from the tee boxes, and an assortment of wiry, practically impregnable rough.

Lee Trevino, who entertains spectators with his golf and his jokes, once told this tale about the plant life at Royal Birkdale: "At fifteen, we put down my bag to hunt for a ball—found the ball, lost the bag." Trevino was kidding. Probably.

Nick Faldo of England definitely lost his share of the lead in the 1983 British Open at Number 12.

Faldo missed the green, made four, and had to wait four years to fulfill his dream of an Auld Open title. Tom Watson, on the other hand, won his first British Open in England at the same championship.

The twelfth hole at Royal Birkdale (right) is sculpted from typical British Open terrain— imposing sandhills, clumps of tortuous heather, mountainous grassy moguls, and an assortment of ugly, wiry rough. Opposite page: Licking the Postage Stamp ought to be easy, but the eighth hole at Royal Troon generally wins more battles than it loses.

© Bob Thomas Sports Photography

Number 8 at Royal Troon
Troon, Scotland
126 yards, par-3

Licking "the Postage Stamp" ought to be easy, golfers must think when studying the shortest hole at Royal Troon.

A wedge, a putt or two…and presto! Par or better.

But then the Firth of Clyde begins a-bubblin', the wind begins a-blowin' mighty like, and this wee hole begins resemblin' the Loch Ness monster.

On windy afternoons at Troon, golfers— pros and amateurs alike—have been seen unsheathing four-irons, and even three-irons, to attack the Postage Stamp.

On windy afternoons at Troon, approach shots to Number 8 regularly land in the heath surrounding the hole or near one of the grassy mounds situated on either side of the miniature green.

Scoring on the hole can be as unpredictable as Scottish weather patterns. When Gene Sarazen was seventy-one, he made one and two, respectively, at the hole during the first two rounds of the 1973 British Open.

Arnold Palmer, golfing god, father of TV golf, made seven there in the second round.

The Postage Stamp looks easy, but often licks its opponents.

Number 17 at St. Andrews Fife, Scotland
461 yards, par-4

The "Road Hole" at St. Andrews is one of the oldest and toughest holes on Earth. Ancient records indicate people have been whacking and chasing golf balls on property comprising the Auld Course since 1552.

The Road Hole has led twenty-three golfers to the British Open championship and many, many more to catastrophe. That is the reputation of hole Number 17.

John H. Taylor, winner of the open five times in the late nineteenth century and early twentieth century, once needed thirteen whacks to play the hole.

Tommy Nakajima of Japan once walked off the green entering a nine onto his scorecard. He was on in two, but the cabal of golfing physics and the sinisterly perfect location of the Road Bunker literally left Nakajima in a hole.

What Nakajima did was putt his golf ball into the sand. He did not reemerge from the hazard until he had taken four swings at the ball.

In the final round of the 1984 British Open, Tom Watson was chasing Sevé Ballesteros, the spirit of Harry Vardon, and golf history before he came to Number 17.

But he struck his second shot too strongly there. The ball skimmed across the green and stopped only when it collided with the old stone wall that separates the gallery from the hole.

Watson was unable to save par. He lost the championship to Ballesteros, along with his opportunity to win his third title in succession, his sixth overall, and match Vardon's record total.

Number 2 at Spyglass Hill
Pebble Beach, California
350 yards, par-4

Above: Sandy wasteland and spikes of impregnable plant life defend the elevated green from adventurous golfers looking to conquer the imposing second hole at Spyglass Hill.

The name of the course comes from the swash-buckling novel *Treasure Island.* Its considerable reputation derives from a collection of horror stories told by Spyglass survivors.

The scary tale that sums up the difficulty of the layout involves two doctors who begin their round with three dozen golf balls, then dispatch the caddie to fetch them a new supply at the end of six holes.

There is no punch line.

Spyglass is tough—probably tougher than its sister course, Pebble Beach at Cypress Point.

The second hole is about 250 yards shorter than the first hole, but making four here is no easier than making five at Number 1.

How best to attack "Billy Bones," the nick-name of the hole, and another tribute to *Treasure Island*?

The fairway is a narrow, dangerous alley, so laying up with a long iron usually is the safest way to avoid the thickets of scrub that catch and often conceal forever wayward golf balls.

Sandy wasteland and spikes of links plant life defend the elevated green from adventurous golfers, who need bravery and apparently an end-less supply of golf balls to outlast Number 2 at Spyglass Hill.

© Allen Steele/Allsport

Number 17 at Tournament Players Course
Ponte Vedra, Florida
132 yards, par-3

The most intimidating golf hole on Earth may be the seventeenth at Sawgrass, because golf balls struck there either land on the green or skid into water.

Golfers aim at an island 132 yards away, offer good wishes and advice to their golf ball, then beseech the golfing gods to be benevolent. Just this once.

The hole would be less petrifying if the island green were as large as Hawaii. But from the tee box it certainly appears to be smaller, narrower, and not as flat as a dart board. You almost need a telescope to see it.

The rolling green rises from a lake, and while the water surrounding it ought to be enough of an obstacle to panic even the most confident golfer, a small bunker on the right supplies one more reason to quit playing the game of golf and take up stationary biking as a more rewarding and productive hobby.

The hole and the remainder of the TPC course are the demented emanations of architect Pete Dye's radical mind.

He created a fearsome layout, a trend, and also plenty of controversy with his original "stadium course," built with the magnanimous goal of providing spectators with unobstructed views of the action from grassy embankments.

The course, particularly the seventeenth hole, is often more sadistic than altruistic, though.

Number 9 at Turnberry (Ailsa Course) Ayrshire, Scotland
455 yards, par-4

One hole at Turnberry is more exquisite than all the others: Number 9.

An old white lighthouse decorates the ninth fairway, but sorrowfully, it offers no guidance to landlubbers or golf lovers.

Golfers unfamiliar with the rolling terrain ought to have some assistance navigating Turnberry, especially in foul weather, the prevailing conditions.

The ninth tee balances on a craggy rockpile, and the first shot needs to clear more jagged topography in order to safely reach the slender fairway made of fescue grass.

On the right is part of an old Spitfire tarmac left over from World War II.

The course was strategic because of its proximity to the ocean, so the Royal Air Force built runways on the fairways during the war to accommodate its Coastal Command. Scottish architect Mackenzie Ross rebuilt the course in the 1970s; nowadays, wild flowers border the runway.

Gorse, bracken, whin, and broom—confusing, irksome, and omnipresent links plant life—cover the fairways and guard the greens.

Golf balls short of the ninth green usually are in better position than golf balls behind the small green, where the gorse grows and muscle-bound shots usually vanish.

Par is an impressive score here, but the scenery is the sedative that soothes agitated golfers jousting Turnberry.

Opposite page: "Golf wasn't meant to be fair," Pete Dye, *architect of the seventeenth hole at the Tournament Players Course, replies gruffly to his critics.* Right: *The impressive lighthouse decorating the background sheds absolutely no light on how to defeat the ninth hole at Turnberry.*

© Bob Thomas Sports Photography

Epilogue

Future of Golf

H E DEPLORES THE CONTAMINATION OF golf by gadgeteers posing as scientists. So, in his golf bag, Gary Player does not carry any woods with metal heads, long putters, or souped-up golf balls that manufacturers essentially pledge will land on the green, and maybe even on Mars.

"I don't know where the game is going," says Player, one of the finest golfers in history. "I have my reservations. There are millions of people attempting to manufacture some golf gadget, some item to make the game more illegal. All the gadgets are changing the nature of the game."

When the game was young, golfers were playful Scottish shepherds chasing wee stanes wi' crookid sticks. Professional golfers nowadays launch "hot" balls into the stratosphere using clubs made with nuclear warheads, instead of standard clubheads.

"I don't believe in 'square grooves.' I don't believe in the ball going farther. I don't believe in metal heads," Player says. "I agree with Greg Norman that the entrants in the tournament all should use the same brand of golf balls, randomly, but personally, chosen from a barrel at the first tee."

Player presents himself as an auld-world golfer detained involuntarily on a square-groove, hot-ball, jumbo-driver, long-putter planet. He does not seek any more progress, nor does he accept any more progress. Meddling further with the game is his idea of mortal sin.

He looks incensed, acts like someone whose winning putt kissed the lip of the cup, and enjoying the sensation, stayed there, when discussing the long putter. The downright silly putter.

Courtesy The Sharper Image

"Orville Moody was, without question, the worst putter I'd seen in all my life," he says. "If you gave him three two-foot putts to win a championship, maybe, just maybe, he'd hit the side of the hole with one of them.

"Then, in 1989, he was (the Senior Tour) Putter of the Year."

The long putter, known as "Slim Jim," "The Broom," or "Soul Pole" among pros, has been a life preserver of sorts for many professional golfers, particularly Moody and other members of the PGA Senior Tour.

Its shaft is sometimes fifty-two inches long, enabling the golfer to stand comfortably above the ball, and the extra length also permits the golfer to anchor the left hand against the chest, effectively removing it from the swing. The right hand pushes the putter in a sweeping motion.

Conventional putters require influence from both hands to work correctly, otherwise the blade will not be square at impact and the ball will roll off line. A conventional putter requires more "touch," a commodity golfers lose with age.

"My nerves aren't as steady as they were ten, fifteen, twenty years ago," Player says, "but I'm not ready for one of those long putters."

He repeats his mantra and his message: "I don't know where the game is going."

"Square grooves" on the club face of irons is another subject that angers Player, causes him to act as though he had been told the Royal and Ancient Golf Club had moved its headquarters from St. Andrews, Scotland, to Jupiter, Florida.

"I can remember times when, say, Ben Hogan overshot the eighteenth green and landed in a trap a few feet behind the hole. The announcers would say: 'There's no way he'll be able to stop the ball near the hole.' I'm talking about *Ben Hogan!*

"But nowadays Joe Blow gets up there with his sand wedge…and the green is slightly down-hill…and Joe Blow swings…and the ball stops…and the announcers start screaming: 'What a great player.'

"Hell, if you've got square grooves, you're not a great player. In my day, you had to open up the club face, use certain hand action to get the ball to stop. That was golf. That was shot making."

Player loves golf, the auld game. The future of the sport may not look much different from its present, though.

In recent international tournaments, European golfers, both male and female, have been playing as if their forefathers and foremothers invented golf.

Okay, ancient Europeans did originate the game. However, American golfers were the kings and queens of clubs until the middle of the 1980s, when the U.S. began losing its death grip on the Masters, the women's U.S. Open, the Walker Cup, the Ryder Cup, and the Curtis Cup.

So how long can golfers from Europe continue to roll on American turf like a perfectly struck putt?

Indefinitely, maybe.

Nick Faldo of England and Spaniard José Marie Olazabal (Ola-THA-bal) appear to be Jack Nicklaus's "Bear Apparents." Liselotte Neumann of Sweden may become the next great female golfer.

Olazabal, twenty-five years old, won the World Series of golf by twelve strokes at Firestone Country Club in 1990, and someday soon will win one of the major championships and replace Sevé Ballesteros or Greg Norman as the dominant global golfer.

He has no intention of settling on the PGA Tour, even though he is exempt from qualifying until the beginning of the twenty-first century because of his victory in the World Series.

"Golf is a world game," Olazabal says. "So a golfer should play all over the world."

Golf also is a much different game than the one ancient Scots originated more than 500 years ago in a cow pasture. Player fears technology will intrude more on the sport and blow it further from its Scottish roots:

"With all the stuff that's coming out, guaranteed, someday, on an uphill hole, a player will say: 'I don't hit the ball that long, switch on that fan behind me.'"

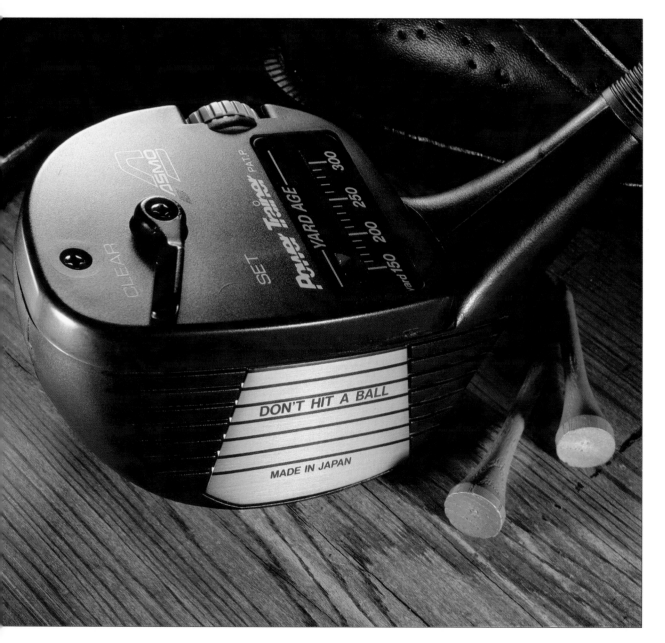

Opposite page: Who knows? In the future, 100-watt golf balls may roll smoothly on rutless, markless artificial turf. Below: Clubs with nuclear warheads and stiff graphite shafts are adding incredible distance to shots, and changing the nature and direction of the game of golf.

Appendix

MAJOR CHAMPIONSHIP TITLISTS

THE MASTERS TOURNAMENT

Year	Name	Score	Year	Name	Score	Year	Name	Score
1934	Horton Smith	284	1956	Jack Burke, Jr.	289	1976	Ray Floyd	271
1935	*Gene Sarazen (144)	282	1957	Doug Ford	283	1977	Tom Watson	276
1936	Horton Smith	285	1958	Arnold Palmer	284	1978	Gary Player	277
1937	Byron Nelson	283	1959	Art Wall, Jr.	284	1979	**Fuzzy Zoeller	280
1938	Henry Picard	285	1960	Arnold Palmer	282	1980	Sevé Ballesteros	275
1939	Ralph Guldahl	279	1961	Gary Player	280	1981	Tom Watson	280
1940	Jimmy Demaret	280	1962	*Arnold Palmer (68)	280	1982	**Craig Stadler	284
1941	Craig Wood	280	1963	Jack Nicklaus	286	1983	Sevé Ballesteros	280
1942	*Byron Nelson (69)	280	1964	Arnold Palmer	276	1984	Ben Crenshaw	277
1943–45	No tournament; World War II		1965	Jack Nicklaus	271	1985	Bernhard Langer	282
1946	Herman Keiser	282	1966	*Jack Nicklaus (70)	288	1986	Jack Nicklaus	279
1947	Jimmy Demaret	281	1967	Gay Brewer, Jr.	280	1987	**Larry Mize	285
1948	Claude Harmon	279	1968	Bob Goalby	277	1988	Sandy Lyle	281
1949	Sam Snead	282	1969	George Archer	281	1989	Nick Faldo	283
1950	Jimmy Demaret	283	1970	*Billy Casper (69)	279	1990	**Nick Faldo	278
1951	Ben Hogan	280	1971	Charles Coody	279			
1952	Sam Snead	282	1972	Jack Nicklaus	286			
1953	Ben Hogan	274	1973	Tommy Aaron	283			
1954	*Sam Snead (70)	289	1974	Gary Player	278		*Winner in play-off, score in parentheses.	
1955	Cary Middlecoff	279	1975	Jack Nicklaus	276		**Winner in sudden-death play-off.	

UNITED STATES OPEN (MEN)

Year	Name	Score	Year	Name	Score	Year	Name	Score
1895	Horace Rawlins	*173	1927	**Tommy Armour (76)	301	1962	**Jack Nicklaus (71)	283
1896	James Foulis	*152	1928	**Johnny Farrell (143)	294	1963	**Julius Boros (70)	293
1897	Joe Lloyd	*162	1929	**Bobby Jones (141)	294	1964	Ken Venturi	278
1898	Fred Herd	328	1930	Bobby Jones	287	1965	**Gary Player (71)	282
1899	Willie Smith	315	1931	**Billy Burke (297)	292	1966	**Billy Casper (69)	278
1900	Harry Vardon	313	1932	Gene Sarazen	286	1967	Jack Nicklaus	275
1901	**Willie Anderson (85)	331	1933	Johnny Goodman	287	1968	Lee Trevino	275
1902	Laurie Auchterlonie	307	1934	Olin Dutra	293	1969	Orville Moody	281
1903	**Willie Anderson (82)	307	1935	Sam Parks, Jr.	299	1970	Tony Jacklin	281
1904	Willie Anderson	303	1936	Tony Manero	282	1971	**Lee Trevino (68)	280
1905	Willie Anderson	314	1937	Ralph Guldahl	281	1972	Jack Nicklaus	290
1906	Alex Smith	295	1938	Ralph Guldahl	284	1973	Johnny Miller	279
1907	Alex Ross	302	1939	**Byron Nelson (138)	284	1974	Hale Irwin	287
1908	**Fred McLeod (77)	322	1940	**Lawson Little (70)	287	1975	**Lou Graham (71)	287
1909	George Sargent	290	1941	Craig Wood	284	1976	Jerry Pate	277
1910	**Alex Smith (71)	298	1942–45	No tournament; World War II		1977	Hubert Green	278
1911	**John McDermott (80)	307	1946	**Lloyd Mangrum (144)	284	1978	Andy North	285
1912	John McDermott	294	1947	**Lew Worsham (69)	282	1979	Hale Irwin	284
1913	**Francis Ouimet (72)	304	1948	Ben Hogan	276	1980	Jack Nicklaus	272
1914	Walter Hagen	290	1949	Cary Middlecoff	286	1981	David Graham	273
1915	Jerome Travers	297	1950	**Ben Hogan (69)	287	1982	Tom Watson	282
1916	Charles Evans, Jr.	286	1951	Ben Hogan	287	1983	Larry Nelson	280
1917	No tournament; World War I		1952	Julius Boros	281	1984	**Fuzzy Zoeller (67)	276
1918	No tournament; World War I		1953	Ben Hogan	283	1985	Andy North	279
1919	**Walter Hagen (77)	301	1954	Ed Furgol	284	1986	Ray Floyd	279
1920	Edward Ray	295	1955	**Jack Fleck (69)	287	1987	Scott Simpson	277
1921	James M. Barnes	289	1956	Cary Middlecoff	281	1988	**Curtis Strange (71)	278
1922	Gene Sarazen	288	1957	**Dick Mayer (72)	282	1989	Curtis Strange	278
1923	**Bobby Jones (76)	296	1958	Tommy Bolt	283	1990	†Hale Irwin	280
1924	Cyril Walker	297	1959	Billy Casper	282			
1925	**W. McFarlane (147)	291	1960	Arnold Palmer	280			
1926	Bobby Jones	293	1961	Gene Littler	281			

*The tournament was 36 holes long until 1898.

**Winner in play-off, score in parentheses.

† Irwin defeated Mike Donald in sudden death in 1990.

BRITISH OPEN

Year	Name	Score	Year	Name	Score	Year	Name	Score
1860	Willie Park	*174	1892	Harold H. Hilton	305	1928	Walter Hagen	292
1861	Tom Morris, Sr.	*163	1893	William Auchterlonie	322	1929	Walter Hagen	292
1862	Tom Morris, Sr.	*163	1894	John H. Taylor	326	1930	Bobby Jones	291
1863	Willie Park	*168	1895	John H. Taylor	322	1931	Tommy D. Armour	296
1864	Tom Morris, Sr.	*160	1896	**Harry Vardon (157)	316	1932	Gene Sarazen	283
1865	Andrew Strath	*162	1897	Harold H. Hilton	314	1933	**Denny Shute (149)	292
1866	Willie Park	*169	1898	Harry Vardon	307	1934	Henry Cotton	283
1867	Tom Morris, Sr.	*170	1899	Harry Vardon	310	1935	Alfred Perry	283
1868	Tom Morris, Jr.	*154	1900	John H. Taylor	309	1936	Alfred Padgham	287
1869	Tom Morris, Jr.	*157	1901	James Braid	318	1937	Henry Cotton	283
1870	Tom Morris, Jr.	*149	1902	Alexander Herd	307	1938	R. A. Whitcombe	295
1871	No championship played		1903	Harry Vardon	300	1939	Richard Burton	290
1872	Tom Morris, Jr.	*166	1904	Jack White	296	1940–45	No championship played	
1873	Tom Kidd	*179	1905	James Braid	318	1946	Sam Snead	290
1874	Mungo Park	*159	1906	James Braid	300	1947	Fred Daly	293
1875	Willie Park	*166	1907	Arnaud Massy	312	1948	Henry Cotton	294
1876	Bob Martin	*176	1908	James Braid	291	1949	**Bobby Locke (135)	283
1877	Jamie Anderson	*160	1909	John H. Taylor	295	1950	Bobby Locke	279
1878	Jamie Anderson	*157	1910	James Braid	299	1951	Max Faulkner	285
1879	Jamie Anderson	*169	1911	Harry Vardon	303	1952	Bobby Locke	287
1880	Robert Ferguson	*162	1912	Ted Ray	295	1953	Ben Hogan	282
1881	Robert Ferguson	*170	1913	John H. Taylor	304	1954	Peter Thomson	283
1882	Robert Ferguson	*171	1914	Harry Vardon	306	1955	Peter Thomson	281
1883	Willie Fernie	*159	1915–19	No championship played		1956	Peter Thomson	281
1884	Jack Simpson	*160	1920	George Duncan	303	1957	Bobby Locke	279
1885	Bob Martin	*171	1921	**Jack Hutchison (150)	296	1958	**Peter Thomson (139)	278
1886	David Brown	*157	1922	Walter Hagen	300	1959	Gary Player	284
1887	Willie Park, Jr.	*161	1923	Arthur G. Havers	295	1960	Kel Nagle	278
1888	Jack Burns	*171	1924	Walter Hagen	301	1961	Arnold Palmer	284
1889	**Willie Park, Jr. (158)	*155	1925	James M. Barnes	300	1962	Arnold Palmer	276
1889	John Ball	*164	1926	Bobby Jones	291	1963	**Bob Charles (140)	277
1891	Hugh Kirkaldy	*166	1927	Bobby Jones	285	1964	Tony Lema	279

Year	Name	Score
1965	Peter Thomson	285
1966	Jack Nicklaus	282
1967	Roberto DeVicenzo	278
1968	Gary Player	289
1969	Tony Jacklin	280
1970	**Jack Nicklaus (72)	283
1971	Lee Trevino	278
1972	Lee Trevino	278
1973	Tom Weiskopf	276
1974	Gary Player	282
1975	**Tom Watson (71)	279
1976	Johnny Miller	279
1977	Tom Watson	268
1978	Jack Nicklaus	281
1979	Sevé Ballesteros	283
1980	Tom Watson	271
1981	Bill Rogers	276
1982	Tom Watson	284
1983	Tom Watson	275
1984	Sevé Ballesteros	276
1985	Sandy Lyle	282
1986	Greg Norman	280
1987	Nick Faldo	279
1988	Sevé Ballesteros	273
1989	†Mark Calcavecchia	275
1990	Nick Faldo	270

*The championship was 36 holes until 1892.

**Winner in play-off, score in parentheses.

†Mark Calcavecchia won a four-hole play-off in 1989.

U.S. Women's Open

Year	Name	Score	Year	Name	Score
1946	Patty Berg	5 and 4	1970	Donna Caponi	287
1947	Betty Jameson	295	1971	JoAnne Carner	288
1948	Babe Zaharias	300	1972	Susie Berning	299
1949	Louise Suggs	291	1973	Susie Berning	290
1950	Babe Zaharias	271	1974	Sandra Haynie	295
1951	Betsy Rawls	293	1975	Sandra Palmer	295
1952	Louise Suggs	284	1976	*JoAnne Carner (76)	292
1953	*Betsy Rawls (70)	302	1977	Hollis Stacy	292
1954	Babe Zaharias	291	1978	Hollis Stacy	289
1955	Fay Crocker	299	1979	Jerilyn Britz	284
1956	*Kathy Cornelius (75)	302	1980	Amy Alcott	280
1957	Betsy Rawls	299	1981	Pat Bradley	279
1958	Mickey Wright	290	1982	Janet Anderson	283
1959	Mickey Wright	287	1983	Jan Stephenson	290
1960	Betsy Rawls	292	1984	Hollis Stacy	290
1961	Mickey Wright	293	1985	Kathy Baker	280
1962	Murle Breer	301	1986	*Jan Geddes (71)	287
1963	Mary Mills	289	1987	*Laura Davies (71)	285
1964	*Mickey Wright (70)	290	1988	Lisolette Neumann	277
1965	Carol Mann	290	1989	Betsy King	278
1966	Sandra Spuzich	297	1990	Betsy King	284
1967	Catherine LaCoste (a)	294			
1968	Susie Bering	289		(a) Amateur	
1969	Donna Caponi	294		*Winner in play-off, score in parentheses.	

GROWTH OF TOUR PURSES

PGA

Year	Number of events	Official purse	Year	Number of events	Official purse
1938	38	$158,000	1965	36	$2,848,515
1939	28	$121,000	1966	36	$3,704,445
1940	27	$117,000	1967	37	$3,979,162
1941	30	$169,200	1968	45	$5,077,600
1942	21	$116,500	1969	47	$5,465,875
1943	3	$17,000	1970	55	$6,751,523
1944	22	$150,500	1971	63	$7,116,000
1945	36	$435,380	1972	71	$7,596,749
1946	37	$411,533	1973	75	$8,657,225
1947	31	$352,500	1974	57	$8,165,941
1948	34	$427,000	1975	51	$7,895,450
1949	25	$338,200	1976	49	$9,157,522
1950	33	$459,950	1977	48	$9,688,977
1951	30	$460,200	1978	48	$10,337,332
1952	32	$498,016	1979	46	$12,801,200
1953	32	$562,704	1980	45	$13,371,786
1954	26	$600,819	1981	45	$14,175,393
1955	36	$782,010	1982	46	$15,089,576
1956	36	$847,070	1983	45	$17,588,242
1957	32	$820,360	1984	46	$21,251,382
1958	39	$1,005,800	1985	47	$25,290,526
1959	43	$1,225,205	1986	46	$25,442,242
1960	41	$1,335,242	1987	46	$32,106,093
1961	45	$1,461,830	1988	47	$36,959,307
1962	49	$1,790,320	1989	44	$41,288,787
1963	43	$2,044,900	1990	51	$52,000,000
1964	41	$2,301,063			

PGA SENIOR

Year	Number of events	Official purse
1980	2	$250,000
1981	5	$750,000
1982	11	$1,372,000
1983	24	$3,364,768
1984	24	$5,156,000
1985	27	$6,076,000
1986	28	$6,300,000
1987	35	$8,700,000
1988	37	$10,500,000
1989	41	$14,195,000
1990	42	$17,950,000

LPGA

Year	Number of events	Official purse	Year	Number of events	Official purse
1950	9	$45,000	1971	21	$558,550
1951	14	$70,000	1972	30	$988,400
1952	21	$150,000	1973	36	$1,471,000
1953	24	$120,000	1974	35	$1,752,500
1954	21	$105,000	1975	33	$1,742,000
1955	27	$135,000	1976	32	$2,527,000
1956	26	$140,000	1977	35	$3,058,000
1957	26	$147,830	1978	37	$3,925,000
1958	25	$158,600	1979	38	$4,400,000
1959	26	$202,500	1980	40	$5,150,000
1960	25	$186,700	1981	40	$5,800,000
1961	24	$288,750	1982	38	$6,400,000
1962	32	$338,450	1983	36	$7,000,000
1963	34	$345,300	1984	38	$8,000,000
1964	33	$351,000	1985	38	$9,000,000
1965	33	$356,316	1986	36	$10,000,000
1966	37	$509,500	1987	36	$11,400,000
1967	32	$435,250	1988	36	$12,510,000
1968	34	$550,185	1989	36	$14,190,000
1969	29	$597,290	1990	36	$17,500,000
1970	21	$435,040			

TOP FIVE VICTORIES

PGA SENIOR (CAREER THROUGH 1990)

Place	Name	No.
1.	Miller Barber	24
2.	Don January	22
3.	Bruce Crampton	17
4.	Chi Chi Rodriguez	16
5.	Gary Player	15

TOP TEN MAJOR TITLEHOLDERS

PGA
(CAREER THROUGH 1990)

1. Jack Nicklaus, 18 (6 Masters, 5 U.S. Opens, 3 British Opens, 4 PGAs)

2. Walter Hagen, 11 (2 U.S. Opens, 4 British Opens, 5 PGAs)

3. (Tie) Gary Player, 9 (3 Masters, 1 U.S. Open, 3 British Opens, 2 PGAs)

   Ben Hogan, 9 (2 Masters, 4 U.S. Opens, 1 British Open, 2 PGAs)

4. Tom Watson, 8 (2 Masters, 1 U.S. Open, 5 British Opens)

5. (Tie) Gene Sarazen, 7 (1 Masters, 2 U.S. Opens, 1 British Open, 3 PGAs)

   Arnold Palmer, 7 (4 Masters, 1 U.S. Open, 2 British Opens)

   Bobby Jones, 7 (4 U.S. Opens, 3 British Opens)

   Sam Snead, 7 (3 Masters, 1 British Open, 3 PGAs)

   Harry Vardon, 7 (1 U.S. Open, 6 British Opens)

TOP TEN MAJOR TITLEHOLDERS

LPGA
(CAREER THROUGH 1990)

1. Patty Berg, 15 (1 U.S. Open, 7 Titleholders, 7 Western Opens)

2. Mickey Wright, 13 (5 LPGAs, 4 U.S. Opens, 2 Titleholders, 3 Western Opens)

3. (Tie) Louise Suggs, 11 (1 LPGA, 2 U.S. Opens, 4 Titleholders, 4 Western Opens)

   Babe Zaharias, 11 (3 U.S. Opens, 4 Titleholders, 4 Western Opens)

4. Betsy Rawls, 8 (2 LPGAs, 4 U.S. Opens, 2 Western Opens)

5. (Tie) Kathy Whitworth, 6 (3 LPGAs, 2 Titleholders, 1 Western Open)

   Pat Bradley, 6 (1 LPGA, 1 U.S. Open, 3 Du Maurier Classics, 1 Nabisco Championship)

6. (Tie) Donna Caponi, 4 (2 LPGAs, 2 U.S. Opens)

   Sandra Haynie, 4 (2 LPGAs, 1 U.S. Open, 1 Du Maurier Classic)

   Hollis Stacy, 4 (2 LPGAs, 1 U.S. Open, 1 Du Maurier Classic)

INDEX

Page numbers in italics refer to captions, illustrations, and sidebars.

METRIC CONVERSIONS

■

inches	x	2.5	=	centimeters
feet	x	30.0	=	centimeters
yards	x	0.9	=	meters
miles	x	1.6	=	kilometers